I Have known  led young man wi the Bible. Larry be is simply devoted ...., His Holy Scriptures. Because of Larry's teaching, I have been in ministry for the past 35 years.

I believe this book, *What I've Learned from Amazing Women in the Bible,* will be a great tool for God to use in His church. My church has several large and small bible studies. I look forward to putting this book to great use.

Frank Vargo, Pastor
Freedom Bible Church
Port Charlotte, FL

As a modern career woman, I find it easy to become consumed with thoughts of work, food preparation, anxiety, child rearing, and household tasks. Reading this book reminded me that many women have struggled with similar challenges, and hearing their stories helps put my situation into perspective. In *What I've Learned from Amazing Women in the Bible,* I was reminded of the power of silent actions. At the end of some days, all I can do is pray. As Larry summed it up, *yes, it seems prayer is inaction, but it's actually a critical part of God's plan of action for us.*

Cindi Stevenson,
Director, Sales Enablement.
Insperity,
Kingwood, TX

It has been a joy to read powerful daily devotions written by Larry Shaffer. He combines the highest commitment to scripture with a unique ability to apply Biblical truth, creating insightful Christ-dependent change in the reader. Therefore, I am thrilled about Larry's new book, *What I've Learned from Amazing Women in the Bible*. Utilizing the same gifting, Larry brings the selective narratives about amazing women in the Bible alive. This book provides the reader or small group with unique insight as well as great Biblical applications and discussion questions.

Matt Brinkley
Founder and Director
of PACT Ministry,
Atlanta, GA

What I've Learned from Amazing Women in the Bible is indeed a thought provoking and thoroughly intriguing perspective of several amazing women in the Bible. Larry Shaffer has done a magnificent job capturing the verses, story and perspective pertaining to each of them. In doing so, he shows their struggles, power and influence on history. Taking those lessons and applying them to our world and lives today requires a level of soul searching which, if done, provides enlightenment and a stronger personal connection to God. Will you take the challenge?

Jalyn Noel
Managing Director,
Innovation & Development
Insperity
Kingwood, TX

I want some credit for browbeating Larry into sharing publicly the daily devotions that he shared with a few of us privately. Now we have a treasure of those devotionals in a book: *What I've Learned from Amazing Women in the Bible*. I respect a man that deals with the pressures of serving in the senior executive team of a multibillion-dollar public company and yet has found a way to share his Pastors' heart. How can you not stop and take a curious pause on what he has learned about the woman heroes of the Bible.

Doug Tatum,
Author, *No Man's Land*
Faculty Member, The Jim Moran School of
Entrepreneurship, Florida State University
Tallahassee, FL

Larry is truly a man of integrity with a heart to serve others. His passion to lead others to Christ is unwavering. He and his beautiful wife are so loving and accepting of people, always seeking out those they can interact with and make them feel loved and accepted. This book, *What I've Learned from Amazing Women in the Bible*, shows his true heart, that people would not only read the word of God but learn how to apply it in their life. I believe this book will be life changing!

Cherish Isaac
Managing Director,
Sales Operations and Development
Insperity
Kingwood, TX

I have known Larry Shaffer for a long time. He is not only a very effective business leader; he is a man who walks with God. He loves God and he loves his Word. *What I've Learned from Amazing Women in the Bible* is a superb tool for individual believers and for small groups in chasing after God!

Jeff Wells
Lead Pastor
WoodsEdge Community Church
The Woodlands, TX

Reading *What I've Learned from Amazing Women in the Bible,* feels like having a conversation with a mentor who has become a friend. He is able to take the narrative from the story and relate it to real life examples of today that make you feel understood.

As a woman on a mission to empower other women, I am so encouraged and grateful that such a strong man of faith chose to write a book about the lessons he learned from women of the Bible. Thank you, Larry and well done."

Leah Glover Hayes
Co-Founder, Her Story of Success
www.herstoryofsuccess.com

What I love about Larry is that he is real! No false pretenses, no hidden agenda, just honesty. And you see that in his devotional book, *What I've Learned from Amazing Women in the Bible*. He helps bring God's Word to us in a real fashion, teaching us how to live our daily lives in a practical way that pleases our Savior. I highly recommend his book!"

Allen Peake
Georgia State Representative 2006–2018
Lifelong buddy of Larry
Macon, GA

Devotionals have flooded the marketplace of Christianity over the past 15 years and all with good intent: to keep our vertical relationship with God centered and growing. However, many seem to be more focused on snippets of inspirational life stories with a few verses attached to them. Larry Shaffer takes devotional reading to the next level using eight real-life women of the Bible to teach us timeless lessons from God's point of view, all within their biblical context, engaging their joys and sorrows and motivating life application. I hope this devotional ignites a renewed hunger for Bible reading and understanding as well as more biblically sound and engaging devotionals."

Jeff Moorehead
Lead Pastor
Christ's Church of Federal Way,
Federal Way, WA

When reading through Larry's work, *What I've Learned from Amazing Women in the Bible,* one is immediately challenged by the vulnerability and honesty – it draws you deeper into a love for the Father and His truth. Larry brings an understanding of history and theology in a way that is accessible and engaging to everyone while leading you into a practical application in your own personal life with God.

Josh Walker
Founder and Director
7More
Spring, TX

WHAT I'VE LEARNED FROM

AMAZING WOMEN

—— OF THE BIBLE ——

LARRY SHAFFER

Printed in the United States
ISBN 978-1-7003-5699-4

To my mother–
The first amazing woman to influence my life,
with gratitude for sharing the gospel with me.

TABLE OF CONTENTS

INTRODUCTION

I never intended to write a book about women. I would've considered that a little odd. So, here's what happened. In December 2015, my pastor challenged me hard to spend time with God and in His Word EVERY DAY. I was resistant. I was telling myself I couldn't do it because of the time constraints of my schedule. He challenged me hard and asked that we mutually text each other each morning a summary of our time in the Word. I finally agreed.

I agreed and this decision changed my life. I began a process of reading through Bible books daily, reflecting and praying and then writing down what I learned. I texted him my summary of my time with God 59 out of the first 60 days. Daily time with God became a habit and now I can't *not* do it.

READ, REFLECT AND WRITE.

As someone in the trenches of life beside you, I would humbly suggest that to get the most out of your Bible reading, you must be just as intentional. I began a daily process, 30 to 60 minutes a day, of reading God's Word, reflecting and praying and then writing what I learned.

Reading and reflecting for my devotions, sporadic as they were, was something I had always done. But writing was new to me and writing has made all the difference in the world. I encourage you to try it.

After three plus years of this process, I discovered I had written thousands and thousands of words about what I had learned from God's Word. I decided that I should compile some of my writings into a book. As I looked back at my writings, it dawned on me that the most compelling biblical characters were women. *I had learned a lot from some of the amazing women of the Bible.* There's a lot us men can learn from women in general. And there's a lot that all of us, male and female, can learn from these amazing women in the Bible.

Not all the lessons are the same length, so some might take a little longer to read. And, if you choose to read more than one devotional at a time, that's fine by me. But my real hope is that these devotional lessons will inspire you to read the Bible yourself more consistently. To have daily time with the Lord.

I will confess to you that reading the Bible EVERY DAY has not always been something that's been easy for me. Probably like you, I lead a pretty busy lifestyle. Yet, I have a core belief that God's Word provides me with the power to live a life that honors God and brings me much joy and fulfillment. So down deep, you most likely want to read His Word. I began to change my statement from "I don't have time" to "How can I make it happen?" Give it a try.

And when? There are pressing job responsibilities, household obligations, family commitments, games to watch, games to play, shows to watch … sound familiar? I have found that I need to plan. Otherwise, there are just too many distractions. So, for me, I must be very intentional about my Bible reading.

I determined that I would read the Bible, prayerfully reflect about what I had read, and write down my discoveries and applications daily.

ACKNOWLEDGMENTS

Writing a book was never something I planned on doing, but this project has been more rewarding than I could ever have imagined.

First and foremost, I would like to thank God. In the process of putting this book together, I realized again and again how powerful, loving, gracious, and good He is. Without God, there simply wouldn't have been a book.

I also want to thank my mother, Gladys Shaffer, for sharing the gospel with me as a child. I still remember sitting on our swing set in the backyard as you led me in prayer to receive Christ as my Lord and Savior. Then you became my role model. Every morning when I arose from bed to go to school, I saw you, sitting in your chair, reading your Bible, and praying for your family.

Finally, special thanks to my lovely bride, Leigh. You have always encouraged me in my love for writing. Several years ago, when I first started to share my devotions with a few friends, you diligently forwarded my writing to everyone you felt would be encouraged by it. You believed in me and wanted me to share my writing with others. Leigh, I love you always and forever!

CHAPTER 1

WHAT'S IN A STORY?

DISCOVERING GOD'S TRUTH IN BIBLE NARRATIVES

God is the original Storyteller—and, as the Bible shows us, God loves to tell a good story. I've been reflecting lately about the purpose of narratives in the scope of God's written revelation to us. The Bible could've been written in commands and directives only. After all, at the end of the day, what really matters is that we act correctly. We are to receive Christ and obey Him. Pretty simple. Just do this and don't do that. The repetition of line upon line, precept upon precept, here a little and there a little, is a simple formula of learning. We should simply obey.

But God gave us something beyond His commands and directives. He gave us stories that especially appeal to people with a particular learning style. God is so good and kind that He has given us in His Word, a revelation of Himself that incorporates a kaleidoscope of color, shape, and texture.

AN ARTIST WITH WORDS

Have you ever met an artist—I mean, a real artist—who works with a different medium than Jesus who created with His words? To me, artists are a strange lot, yet I have a very dear friend who is an artist. His attention to the detail of color, contrast, and other crazy artistic nuances is amazing to me. I'm a bottom-line kind of guy. We have nothing in common except our love for the Lord. I learn so much from him. He sees the world differently than I do. He hangs out with non-Christian artists, and he is able to touch them and reach them. They wouldn't trust me for a second.

Our God is a poetic Artist who expresses His emotions in a variety of rich, colorful shades. As we'll discover in this book, God paints pictures in His narratives with an eye for tremendous detail of color, contrast, irony, fear, humor, nuance, and purpose. He's an amazingly artistic Writer. And because He is God, His stories are packed with meaning, and they are perfectly consistent with the messages of all the other forms of His writing such as poetry, prophecy, law, love letters, and epistles. The different genres found in Scripture flawlessly support each other. What a wonder God's Word is!

For example, have you ever thought about the following?

- The shepherd boy David picked up five smooth stones, but only needed one to defeat Israel's enemy, the giant Goliath. David was skilled and precise with his sling, and by God's providence a single stone penetrated the exact point of Goliath's weakness and killed him (1 Samuel 17).

- When He was in the wilderness being tempted by Satan, Jesus—in a sense—picked up the five books of Moses to battle the enemy. Genesis, Exodus, Leviticus, Numbers, and Deuteronomy are the five books of Moses, but when Jesus was tempted, He only used one of them. Three times Satan tempted Jesus, and every time Jesus responded with "It is written." Every time Jesus quoted the book of Deuteronomy. Jesus needed only one of the five stones available to Him. Jesus was precise with His use of Scripture, always addressing the specific weakness of Satan's temptation (Matthew 4:1-11).

- Later, Paul taught about using "the sword of the Spirit, which is the word of God," in our spiritual battle with Satan (Ephesians 6:17). The Greek word for *sword* does not refer to the big sword of ancient battles. This Ephesians 6:17 weapon is a dagger. Also, the Greek for the *word of God* is not the full scope of Scripture; it is instead a specific phrase. So, just like David in his battle with Goliath and just like Jesus in His temptation from Satan, we are taught by Paul to be skilled with our dagger and be precise in our battle against Satan's particular temptations. We are not to just throw the whole Bible at Satan. Instead, just as if we were using a dagger to penetrate a vital organ, we are to use specific and precise Scriptures to stand strong against Satan's temptations.

God gave us an Old Testament narrative, a scene from Jesus' life and a teaching from the apostle Paul, that correlate perfectly to enlighten, delight, and instruct us in how to fight our spiritual battle with Satan. That's just cool! What a gift God has given us in His Word!

WHY DID GOD CHOOSE NARRATIVES?

About three years ago, after many years of focusing on the New Testament, I turned my attention to Old Testament narratives. It has been quite a rewarding journey into the Old Testament, and that makes me want to explore it more.

So, why do you suppose God uses narrative to communicate His truth? Narratives—stories—comprise nearly half of the Old Testament. The first five books of the New Testament are narratives, so it's obviously an important and effective literary style. I believe God chose narratives as a primary means of communicating His story and key theological truth for several reasons:

- Narratives are an interesting way to teach children and adults important truths about God.

- Narratives draw us into the action and the plot.

- Narratives depict real life and can heighten interest because the reader can relate to the characters.

- Narratives are easy to remember and pass on.

- God often includes Himself in the story and can therefore teach us how He views the issues of life.

- Bible narratives aren't like Facebook where the author only presents positive stories. Bible narratives usually tell the ugly side of the situation as well as the triumphs.

- Bible narratives are not random stories; they are stories that teach. In addition, all the narratives fit perfectly together within the whole story of God.

My goal is not just to tell you what I'm learning from the Bible but also to encourage you to gain more from your own personal journey through the Bible. When we read and consider biblical narratives, we should not only enjoy the story, but with discernment, we should also draw out the principles and the theological truth that God intended to communicate.

HOW DO I APPROACH NARRATIVES?

As we approach the narrative, we should begin with the understanding that there are always primary truths and secondary truths. Part of the fun is trying to discover God's main purpose for including each story in Scripture and for mentioning each detail contained within the narrative. In order to gain the optimal blessings of God's Word in our lives, we should be committed to, and diligent about, handling God's Word accurately.

When I'm reading and studying the Bible, a verse that often floats into my consciousness is 2 Timothy 2:15:

Be diligent to present yourself approved to God as a workman who does not need to be ashamed, accurately handling the word of truth.

Interestingly, the verse before and after this one tells the reader to not get involved in useless arguments and to avoid *worldly and empty chatter* (verse 16). Instead, we are to give our attention to accurately and diligently handling the Word because, after all, it *is* the Word of God!

So let's not handle God's Word the way I handle classic rock music. I especially love the Beatles. When I listen to the simple and enjoyable melody of "With a Little Help from My Friends," I choose not to consider those "friends" as a reference to drugs, which was most likely the author's original intent. Instead, I consider it a simple tribute to true friends. I suppose that's a little silly, but I love the Beatles music, so I choose not to give too much thought to the original intent.

Sadly—and at great risk—many people choose to give little attention to the original intent of certain Bible passages and simply derive meaning according to what they want Scripture to say. This approach is biblical malpractice. Instead, we should prayerfully and diligently work to discover the passage's main point and purpose. So, the question is not, "What does this passage mean *to me*?" but rather, "What does this passage *mean*?" Once we understand the original intent and main teaching, then we should ask, "What does it mean to me?" in the sense of "What is God telling me to do in this passage?"

Father, we are grateful that You are a communicator and that You have given us in Your Book a variety of genres to enjoy and learn from. Thank You for blessing us with this wondrous Book filled with stories, poems, instruction, and prophecy to teach us, lead us, and give us hope. Help us, by Your guidance, to explore all its truth. Give us insight into all Your Word so that we might live in fullness and joy and ultimate victory in all things. Amen!

CHAPTER 2

HANNAH: OPPRESSED IN SPIRIT

LESSON 1
Pain and Triumph

1 Samuel 1: 1-15

Now there was a certain man ... and his name was Elkanah ... He had two wives; the name of one was Hannah and the name of the other Peninnah; and Peninnah had children, but Hannah had no children....

When the day came that Elkanah sacrificed, he would give portions to Peninnah, his wife, and to all her sons and her daughters; but to Hannah he would give a double portion, for he loved Hannah, but the LORD had closed her womb....

Greatly distressed, [Hannah] prayed to the LORD and wept bitterly. She made a vow and said, "O LORD of Hosts, if You will indeed look on the affliction of Your maidservant and remember me, and not forget Your maidservant, but will give Your maidservant a son, then I will give him to the LORD all the days of his life"...

> *Now it came about, as she continued praying before the*
> *Lord, that Eli [the priest] was watching her mouth. As*
> *for Hannah, she was speaking in her heart, only her*
> *lips were moving... Then Eli said to her, "How long will*
> *you make yourself drunk? Put away your wine from*
> *you." But Hannah replied, "No, my lord, I am a woman*
> *oppressed in spirit; I have drunk neither wine nor strong*
> *drink, but I have poured out my soul before the Lord."*
> 1 Samuel 1:1-2, 4-5, 10-15

A MONUMENTAL STORY OF PROMISE AND FULFILLMENT

Who really keeps promises these days? I mean, *really*?

Who keeps their word when no one is watching, or when no one else will know? Whom do you trust to do what they say they will do over the long-term? What about when keeping their promise becomes inconvenient? Or when the situation changes or other obligations arise? Hopefully, you have a few of these people in your life. They are precious!

In the book of 1 Samuel, God makes promises to both Saul and David. God keeps those promises, and He keeps them forever.

Through all the drama, intrigue, deception, defiance, and selfishness that we find in this book of 1 Samuel, God keeps His promises to both Saul and David. For Saul, the promises are not so fun. For David, they are blessings beyond the wildest dreams of the wildest dreamer.

But before God's Word takes us through the lives of Saul and David, the opening chapter of 1 Samuel introduces us to a most amazing woman. Her name is Hannah, and she is a faithful servant of God who keeps her promises.

I really love the story of Hannah. When it comes to character, integrity, grit, and passion, Hannah blows away the other important people we meet in 1 Samuel. She is simply awesome!

The key characters involved in the story of Hannah are:

- Hannah, the mother of Samuel

- Elkanah, Hannah's beloved husband and father of Samuel

- Peninnah, Elkanah's second wife

- Eli, the priest

- Samuel, the son of Hannah and future priest

Chapter 1 provides the backstory of Samuel's birth. His mother, Hannah, is greatly loved by her husband, Elkanah. You would love her too. She is a treasure. But God closes her womb, so Elkanah marries a woman named Peninnah. Seems like a boneheaded decision to me, yet in an agrarian society, men need children if the family is to thrive, and sometimes just survive. Nevertheless, taking a second wife is a faithless and stupid decision.

The second wife is not nice, and she becomes bitter, insecure, and jealous of Hannah whom Elkanah so clearly loves. The fact that Elkanah has only married Peninnah for her body—to bear children—doesn't endear him to Peninnah. She has many children, pleasing her husband but not increasing his love for her. Peninnah sees that Elkanah is utterly head over heels for Hannah. He loves Hannah greatly.

So Wife #2 ridicules Hannah for being barren. Not exactly the Cleaver household. (That's a reference to the TV series *Leave It to Beaver*. Check it out on Netflix if you're too young to know this show!) Her inability to have children is terribly painful to Hannah, but the text states that *the LORD had closed her womb* (1 Samuel 1:5). Clearly, God had a plan.

LEARNING ALERT

As is often the case today, God's plan for His children includes certain pain and distress that He uses to teach and grow us. The intended outcome is a stronger yet humbler follower of God.

Some say that God only brings about good things, and Satan and/or natural circumstances cause pain and distress. This study of Amazing Women clearly shows, however, that God is the Architect of all that happens, and He uses both pain and joy to accomplish His purposes and develop His servant's character.

Some people don't like that last sentence, and they've told me so. However, there is purpose in pain. Physical pain, mental anguish, and broken hearts are difficult trials to endure. They sometimes tempt us toward bitterness. But God promises to carry us through such trials, and He emboldens our faith to trust rather than faint. He is able! If you're hurting, I hope you believe that.

HANNAH IS A SHINING STAR

Hannah is hurting, and we can learn from how she handles it. Specifically, Hannah turns to God in prayer and petition. She goes into the temple, weeping, and pours her heart out before the Lord as she asks Him for a son. In her prayers, she commits to dedicating her son to the Lord. The priest, Eli—seeing *only her lips...moving, but her voice was not heard* (verse 13)—thinks Hannah is drunk. Assuring Eli she isn't drunk, she tells him of her plight and her petition to God. Eli blesses her and prays for her.

Shortly thereafter, Hannah becomes pregnant with Samuel, whose name means "heard by God." Samuel was born according to God's sovereign plan, and He strengthened Hannah's faith through her pain.

Hannah now prepares to give her son fully back to God. She made that promise, and Hannah keeps her promise.

Would Hannah's devotion to the Lord and faithfulness to her promise have happened if she had easily conceived early in her marriage? Maybe, but maybe not. When she was barren, God seemed far from her, but the opposite was actually true. God was near, and He was working out His plan. He was forging Hannah's character and preparing her for a blessing of great magnitude.

There is purpose in pain.

LEARNING ALERT

If only we would believe that God is at work in our lives when it seems He has abandoned us....

The truth is, Jesus said, *"I will never leave you nor forsake you"* (Hebrews 13:5 ESV). Hannah can teach us about trust and faith in a sovereign God who is wise, loving, all-powerful, and close to us even when He seems far away.

We can also learn much from Hannah and her passionate prayers. Yes, God may allow us to go through pain, but that doesn't mean we take it lying down. Hannah goes to God and prays for His physical blessings upon her—and she doesn't let go. God cares about our spiritual state, yes, but He cares about every other aspect of our lives as well. Let's learn from Hannah's passionate and unrelenting prayers to God asking Him to make things good and right in her life.

Using Hannah as an example, Lord, teach us about faith and trust in You! Help us see that You aren't far away even when it feels like it. Grow our faith to go beyond our feelings and help us rest in the promises of Your Word. Remind us of the mighty deeds You have performed in the past. Remind us that our current difficulties are not difficult to You. You are able, and You will bring Your perfect plan to pass! All praise be to You, our mighty God and King! Amen!

Discussion Questions

1. Describe a time in your life when God seemed far from you. What did you do to cope?

2. When you look back (and it may be too soon to do so), what was your sovereign, loving God doing in your life during that time? What was God teaching you?

3. What, if anything, has prompted you to pour out your heart and soul before God? Talk about that experience.

LESSON 2
She's the Real Deal

1 Samuel 1:24-28

> *Now when [Hannah] had weaned [Samuel], she took him up with her, with a three-year-old bull and one ephah of flour, and a jug of wine and brought him to the house of the Lord in Shiloh, although the child was young. Then they slaughtered the bull and brought the boy to Eli. She said, "O my lord! As your soul lives, my lord, I am the woman who stood here beside you, praying to the LORD. For this boy I prayed, and the LORD has given me my petition, which I asked of Him. So I have also dedicated him to the Lord; as long as he lives, he is dedicated to the LORD." And he worshiped the LORD there.*
> 1 Samuel 1:24-28

At the end of chapter 1, after Samuel has been weaned, Hannah takes Samuel back to the priest, Eli, and dedicates him to the Lord for a lifetime of service.

As she walks toward the temple, I wonder if Hannah is tempted to pull back on her previous commitment. Does she have second thoughts about completely dedicating Samuel to the Lord's service as a priest? Maybe he could serve God closer to home. And, to keep her promise, does Hannah really have to give Samuel over for full-time service for his entire life? Sometimes when we make promises out of desperation, we later regret it and sometimes look for ways to compromise or justify a change of plans. Not so with Hannah. Hannah is absolutely faithful to her word.

This visit to the temple is quite different from Hannah's previous trip. Consider the contrasts in Hannah's prayers. In 1 Samuel 1:10, Hannah made a desperate plea to God: *She, greatly distressed, prayed to the LORD and wept bitterly.* Contrast this prayer with Hannah's prayer in 1 Samuel 2:1:

> *Then Hannah prayed and said,*
>   *"My heart exults in the LORD;*
>   *My horn is exalted in the LORD,*
>   *My mouth speaks boldly against my enemies,*
>   *Because I rejoice in Your salvation."*

We can learn a lot regarding prayer from this amazing woman. Hannah's situation changed, and her prayers changed accordingly. But she was authentic in both.

There's much talk in Christian circles today about being authentic. There's value to authenticity, but I sense it gets twisted at times. Sometimes Christians use their stance on authenticity as a license or justification for their sin, their weaknesses, their fleshly propensities. They might say, "I'm just being myself." Let's be careful with that attitude.

LEARNING ALERT

I don't want this false view of authenticity to alter what I see in Hannah as authenticity before God in prayer. When I sink low with feelings of fear and pain, I should take them before God. In our weakness, we should be authentic before God. That's what Hannah did when she was both sad and happy.

Over my many years on this earth, I have found that authenticity seems to come more easily to women than to men. Do you find that to be true? This might be an interesting discussion to have with a few trusted confidants.

Since I've long been a corporate executive, my wife and I have attended many social functions over the years. Sometimes in these settings, we split up and have separate conversations with various small groups. After the party, when my wife and I are talking, she will say, for instance, "Why didn't you tell me that Joe and Kim are having a baby?"

Why? Because Joe, one of my coworkers, never told me his wife was pregnant. So I tell my wife, "I didn't know."

The look on her face is priceless. "You work with Joe every day, and you didn't know? What kind of friend are you?"

I smile, and she smiles and shakes her head.

My wife can find out more about my work associates in one hour at a social function than I will find out in six months at the office. She has a way of caring and asking questions that, with the demands of work, I just don't get around to every day. She has a way of making a person feel it's safe to be authentic. I don't always have that gift.

So, yes, I may make excuses about focusing on work and not being transparent and authentic in my corporate life. But when it comes to God, I need to be authentic! I shouldn't and don't treat God like one of the guys. I should and I must bear my heart and soul before Him. I don't need to hang my dirty laundry out so everyone else sees it, but I should before God. He knows it all anyway. Being authentic draws us toward Him!

We can learn much from Hannah.

Help us, Lord, to be authentic before You. Not as justification for our weaknesses and sin, but as surrender to You with honest pleadings for Your help. Lord, hear us, revive us, restore us, and answer us according to Your perfect will. And in times of joy may we—like Hannah—loudly and boldly exalt You! May we praise You always. Amen!

Discussion Questions

1. What does dedicating our children to the Lord look like in the 21st century? Be specific.

2. Do you ever hold back your feelings in prayer to God? Why or why not? Should you always be totally honest with God? Explain your answer.

LESSON 3
The Beauty of a Godly Woman

1 Samuel 2:1-3

> *Then Hannah prayed and said,*
> *"My heart exults in the LORD;*
> *My horn is exalted in the LORD,*
> *My mouth speaks boldly against my enemies,*
> *Because I rejoice in Your salvation.*
> *There is no one holy like the LORD,*
> *Indeed, there is no one besides You,*
> *Nor is there any rock like our God....*
> *For the LORD is a God of knowledge,*
> *And with Him actions are weighed."*
> 1 Samuel 2:1-3

Don't miss the opening three words of our passage today: *Then Hannah prayed*—and what a prayer it is! Hannah doesn't just wake up one morning and have within her soul the capacity to pray such a prayer. No doubt she has been seeking God and pouring her heart out to Him for many years.

The depth of her prayers is one of the many reasons I believe she is an amazing woman from whom I can learn much. She is a woman of spiritual substance, and such substance doesn't come easily or quickly. Her heart for God has developed over many years of both adversity and joy, and in all circumstances, Hannah prays.

Samuel is born as a result of Hannah praying through one of those times of adversity. Because she is barren, she pleads from the bottom of her heart for God to give her a son, and she commits her son to lifetime ministry should God answer her prayers.

God does answer her prayers, and Hannah celebrates Samuel's birth by praising God with the amazing song of thanksgiving found in 1 Samuel 2:1-11. Once Samuel is weaned, Hannah and Elkanah take him to the temple and leave him with Eli, the priest, to be trained in ministry and leadership.

Samuel stays with Eli in what we would describe as a boarding school, this one specifically for future priests, and his parents visit him periodically throughout the year. So, when Hannah asked God to give her a son and promised to dedicate that son to Him, she knew that keeping her promise would mean physical separation from her young son.

Hannah's commitment is costly, but God has used trials to prepare her and strengthen her. God also has a plan for Samuel. We see, for instance, the sovereignty of God in the formation of Samuel's character, and he in turn becomes an agent of the formation of God's chosen people, Israel.

HANNAH'S PROPHECY

Hannah's prayer of thanksgiving, as she surrenders Samuel to the Lord in the temple, is exultant praise. At the same time it is an amazing song of deep theological truth that includes prophetic words about what God is going to do in Israel during Samuel's time of leadership and beyond.

LEARNING ALERT

Hannah may not be a prophet like Isaiah or Ezekiel, but God uses her to articulate profound truth. Her prayer is so profound, God chose to include it in the Bible. These 11 verses are well worth reading. You don't have to be powerful, charismatic, or have an elevated position to be used by God. God uses the humble servants, male and female, who devote their hearts to prayer with praise and thanksgiving.

HANNAH IS MY HERO!

The theme of Hannah's prayer is that God blesses the humble and weak and exalts them, while crushing those who spurn Him and trust in their own power and wealth. Hannah is prophesying what will be the state of the small nation of Israel throughout history among the powerful and fierce nations that surround them. Even today, powerful nations and religions vow to destroy Israel, just like Goliath vowed to destroy the shepherd boy, David. But they are destined to fail.

Here are a few lines from Hannah's prayer. She may be a simple, Hebrew woman, but when she prays, she becomes a prophetic powerhouse. She prays:

- That *the bows of the mighty are shattered, but the feeble gird on strength* (1 Samuel 2:4)

- That God *keeps the feet of His godly ones, but the wicked ones are silenced in darkness; for not by might shall a man prevail* (verse 9)

- That "*those who contend with the LORD will be shattered...and He will give strength to His king [David]... and will exalt the horn of His anointed* "(verse 10)

- That *the pillars of the earth are the LORD's and He set the world on them* "(verse 8)

HOW, THEN, SHOULD WE LIVE?

We can learn much from Hannah, from both her example and her prophetic song. She is well grounded in her understanding of God, His attributes, and how He deals with people. As we see in Hannah's life, God blesses the humble and stands against the proud. This firm foundational truth helps Hannah rise above her rival's criticism and mocking. I challenge you to follow Hannah's example and consider often the awesome attributes of God. A strong view of God will enhance how you live.

Lord, may we reject the ways of this world and its invitation to glory in a position of power and wealth. May we forsake the pursuit of earthly gain, the praise of others, and the desire to be someone special in the world's eyes. Instead, may we humble ourselves before You and surrender all to You. Amen!

LARRY SHAFFER

Discussion Questions

1. Name a humble person you know—or know of—who is characterized by Christian humility. What is unique about them?

2. What phrase from Hannah's prayer caught your attention?

3. What does 1 Samuel 2:9—*For not by might shall a man prevail*—mean? What encouragement does this verse offer you?

CHAPTER 3

ABIGAIL: STRENGTH AND RESOLVE

LESSON 4
Abigail to the Rescue

1 Samuel 25

> *Now there was a man in Maon whose business was in Carmel; and the man was very rich, and he had three thousand sheep and a thousand goats. And it came about while he was shearing his sheep in Carmel (now the man's name was Nabal, and his wife's name was Abigail). And the woman was intelligent and beautiful in appearance, but the man was harsh and evil in his dealings, and he was a Calebite. David heard in the wilderness that Nabal was shearing his sheep.*
>
> *So David sent ten young men; and David said to the young men, "Go up to Carmel, visit Nabal and greet him in my name; and thus you shall say, 'Have a long life, peace be to you, and peace be to your house, and peace*

LARRY SHAFFER

*be to all that you have. Now I have heard that you have
shearers; now your shepherds have been with us and we
have not insulted them, nor have they missed anything
all the days they were in Carmel. Ask your young men
and they will tell you. Therefore, let my young men find
favor in your eyes, for we have come on a festive day.
Please give whatever you find at hand to yours and to
your son David."*
1 Samuel 25:2-8

These lines are the beginning of a truly amazing story. We
will meet an evil bonehead of a man and a most beautiful
and intelligent woman. We will also see David digress from
his noble actions in the previous chapter when he spared
Saul's life. Once again, women rule, men drool.

TWO HOT-HEADED MEN WALK
INTO A BAR ...

A wealthy man named Nabal owns 3,000 sheep and 1,000
goats that wander into the wilderness area where David
and his men camp out, in hiding from King Saul. Some of
Nabal's men tend to the sheep, but apparently not enough to
keep all the livestock safe. David and his men take it upon
themselves to help the men. The entire time they guard
Nabal's sheep against predators and thieves, David's men
trust that the owner will at some point grant them kindness
and reward them with provisions.

When it's time for Nabal to sheer his sheep, David
sends a few of his men to request provisions from him. The

text introduces Nabal and his wife Abigail in this way: *the woman was intelligent and beautiful in appearance, but the man was harsh and evil in his dealings* (verse 3).

WHAT IS NABAL'S RESPONSE TO DAVID'S MEN?

> *Nabal answered David's servants and said, "Who is David? And who is the son of Jesse? There are many servants today who each are breaking away from his master. Shall I then take my bread and my water and my meat that I have slaughtered for my shearers, and give it to men whose origins I do not know?"*
> 1 Samuel 25:10-11

Nabal rudely states that he doesn't know who David is and that he has no intention of giving *anything* to men he doesn't know. The text indicates that Nabal's men have told him of the kindness and protection David had provided them, but Nabal doesn't care.

HE SAID WHAT???

When David hears about Nabal's response, he is infuriated and vows to take full revenge on Nabal, his household, and all his servants. He would leave no one alive! And, yes, this is the same David who previously refused to take Saul's life into his own hands and left revenge to the Lord.

In Scripture, the volatility of David's humanness is always before us. Yet later in this chapter we'll see why David is called a man after God's own heart. But for now, we have two hot-headed men on a collision course that will be a life-and-death showdown for many innocent people. Who will intervene?

God sends a woman.

LEARNING ALERT

Like David, we make mistakes. Our first thought about a situation may not be the best thought. So, as we journey through life, may we do what God wants us to do. May we increase in wisdom and learn to live more in line with His standards of behavior.

Living a godly life often means not returning anger for anger, and that's hard to do. God tells us not to lean on our own understanding, but to trust in His guidance (see Proverbs 3:5-6). When we do that, our light shines in our homes, our neighborhoods, and our workplaces.

Lord, we're reminded that Your gifts of love and grace are not dependent on our perfect decisions or consistent God-honoring actions. Like David, we are human. When we stray into jealousy, anger, revenge, evil intent, and foolishness, may we quickly come to our senses and surrender our emotions to You. Amen!

Discussion Questions

1. Tell of a time when someone was rude and evil to you? Did you respond like David? Why or why not?

2. When you've felt unappreciated for work you completed in good faith, what was your response? In what ways did that response please God?

3. What is a godly response to rudeness? To someone ripping off you or a loved one?

LESSON 5
Bloodshed Prevented

1 Samuel 25

> *But one of [Nabal's] young men told Abigail, Nabal's wife,*
> *"Behold, David sent messengers from the wilderness to*
> *greet our master, and he scorned them. Yet the men were*
> *very good to us, and we were not insulted, nor did we miss*
> *anything as long as we went about with them, while we*
> *were in the fields. They were a wall to us both by night*
> *and by day, all the time we were with them tending the*
> *sheep. Now therefore, know and consider what you should*
> *do, for evil is plotted against our master and against all his*
> *household; and he is such a worthless man that no one can*
> *speak to him."*
> 1 Samuel 25:14-17

Here's the scene. A rich sheepherder named Nabal speaks disrespectfully about David to his messengers. Learning of this, David and his men set out to wipe out this man, his family, and all his servants. Filled with anger and vengeance, David is heading straight into some good old-fashioned sinful disobedience. David is wrong, but Nabal—a selfish, foolish, and ignorant man—has brought this upon himself.

However, there is one rational and wise person in this story. Thank God for Abigail, Nabal's wife. She is the story's superstar—intelligent, resourceful, honorable, persuasive, and *beautiful in appearance* (verse 3). Pretty much the total package. How did a schmuck like Nabal land such a beautiful and intelligent woman?

A FUNNY THING HAPPENED ON THE WAY TO NABAL'S HOUSE

With two hot-headed men on a collision course toward destruction, God sends a woman!

Nabal's servants hear that David and his men are on their way to seek vengeance. They know that Nabal is a *worthless man that no one can speak to* (verse 17), so they go to Abigail. Without informing or including her husband (I hear that wives do that on occasion), she and her workers immediately gather provisions and set out to meet David and his men.

When Abigail meets up with David, he is still fuming with anger. She dismounts and bows before him. In this case, the fact that David is a sucker for a pretty face works in her favor. Abigail's beauty may have caused David to pause, but it is her words that change everything.

> *When Abigail saw David, she hurried and dismounted from her donkey, and fell on her face before David and bowed herself to the ground. She fell at his feet and said, "On me alone, my lord, be the blame. And please do not let my lord pay attention to this worthless man, Nabal, for as his name is, so is he. Nabal is his name and folly is with him; but, I your maidservant, did not see the young men of my lord whom you sent."*
> 1 Samuel 25:23-25

CHOICE WORDS MELT ANGER AWAY

A brilliant negotiator, Abigail speaks sincerely, eloquently, and persuasively. First, she surprises David by taking full responsibility for her husband's rude behavior: *On me alone, my lord, be the blame.... Please do not pay attention to the worthless man, Nabal... I, your maidservant, did not see the men you sent"* (verses 24-25).

When a person takes full responsibility for a situation, that action has a way of melting anger and tension. That's what happens here. Abigail takes David's attention off Nabal, and David's rage begins to diminish. Then Abigail makes a statement that must have been like a wake-up call to David:

> *Since the LORD has restrained you from shedding blood and from avenging yourself by your own hand, now then let your enemies and those who seek evil against my lord, be as Nabal. Now let this gift, which your maidservant has brought to my lord, be given to the young men who accompany my lord. Please forgive the transgression of your maidservant; for the LORD will certainly make for my lord an enduring house, because my lord is fighting the battles of the LORD, and evil will not be found in you all your days.*
> 1 Samuel 25:26-28

Abigail knows the biblical principle of leaving revenge to the Lord. David has adhered to this principle: when Saul was before him in the cave, David spared his life. Here, Abigail simply reminds David of what he knows. Appealing to his conscience she encourages him to follow biblical law. Then, without hesitating, she asks for forgiveness: *"Please forgive the transgression of your maidservant, for the LORD will certainly make for my lord [David] an enduring house... and evil will not be found in you all your days"* (verse 28).

David's heart is melting! With her carefully chosen words, Abigail keeps him from falling into evil. In verse 32 David says to Abigail, *"Blessed be the LORD God of Israel who sent you this day to meet me, and blessed be your discernment, and blessed be you, who have kept me this day from bloodshed and from avenging myself by my own hand."*

So how does all this drama end? Ten days later God strikes Nabal dead, and David later marries Abigail ... and they live happily ever after. Well, not exactly. Nabal does die, and David does marry Abigail—but happily ever after? Abigail is solid as a rock. David, on the other hand, is a volatile mess. See 1 and 2 Samuel for the full story.

HOW, THEN, SHOULD WE LIVE?

Jesus calls us to be peacemakers—as Abigail was. We are allowed to be angry, but we are to sin not (Ephesians 4:26). We are to leave justice to God (Romans 12:19).

Our world is full of injustice and hypocrisy, evidence of the downward spiral initiated when sin entered the earth. Life will never be fair this side of heaven, yet our mandate is to live the way God expects us to live regardless of what others do in response or how they treat us.

Lord, Abigail is truly a woman of excellence. May we apply the principles of positive influence that she models. May we be peacemakers, encouraging others to avoid sin and bad decisions. As Your servants, may we allow Your Word to increase our wisdom. Help us live with discernment and humility in our daily interactions with others—all for Your glory. Amen!

Discussion Questions

1. What do you like most about Abigail's words, approach, plan, and/or character? Be specific.

2. What, if anything, should Abigail have done differently? What would have been the possible outcome with that change? Or what is the implication if you can't think of anything she could have done better?

3. Tell of someone in your life who acted like Abigail—who acted as a peacemaker, who took the fall for someone else, and/or who humbled herself and asked forgiveness. In what ways was this person's impact on the situation similar to Abigail's influence? Be specific.

CHAPTER 4

THE WOMAN AT THE WELL:
BREAKING TRADITION

LESSON 6
The Woman at the Well

John 4 :7-42

> *There came a woman of Samaria to draw water. Jesus said to her, "Give me a drink...." Therefore, the Samaritan woman said to Him, "How is it that You, being a Jew, ask me for a drink since I am a Samaritan woman?"' ... So the woman left her water pot, and went into the city and said to the men, "Come, see a man who told me all the things that I have done; this is not the Christ, is it?"' They went out of the city and were coming to Him.*
> John 4:7-9 and 28-30

In John 3, Jesus talks with a great teacher of Israel, a highly regarded Pharisee named Nicodemus. Shortly thereafter, Jesus has a conversation with a Samaritan woman who has been married five times and is currently living with a man. What a contrast between these two individuals!

In both interactions, Jesus uses an object lesson to teach rich spiritual truth. With Nicodemus, Jesus speaks of being born again. To the Samaritan woman, He speaks of a well of living water. In both cases, Jesus makes it known that life and heaven are available to all, and that the religious elite do not have an exclusive path to God. Instead, *God so loves the world [all people and all nations] ... that whoever believes will have eternal life* (John 3:16).

Consider now some interesting similarities and differences between Nicodemus and the Samaritan woman:

- The text gives us the Pharisee's name, but not the woman's.

- Nicodemus is well known among the Jews as a great teacher. The woman is a downtrodden and despised nobody.

- Jesus uses an object lesson to teach both of them spiritual principles—and both completely misunderstand.

- In both cases, Jesus ignores their initial superficial questions and comments but instead addresses their real spiritual needs.

- Nicodemus tells no one of his conversation with Jesus, for he has a lot to lose. The woman tells everyone, and many people come to see and speak with Jesus. In fact, *many of the Samaritans believed in Him because of the word of the woman who testified* (John 4:39).

- So who was actually the great teacher—Nicodemus or the woman?

So whom does God use to do great things for His kingdom? I often think of Joseph and Daniel who were pillars of discipline and stable, godly character. But we see in the Bible that God uses many people who were actually moral failures at almost every level. Does God simply have a twisted sense of humor?

- Noah demonstrates his solid faith in God before and during the flood, but shortly after exiting the ark, Noah is found naked and drunk.

- Samson and David are huge moral failures.

- Rahab is a harlot by trade.

- Ruth is a Moabite idol worshipper.

- Zacchaeus is an extortionist and tax collector.

- James and John have their mother ask if they could be honored above the other disciples and sit on Jesus' right and left hands in glory.

- The disciples often argue over who is the greatest among them.

- Peter denies even knowing Christ after promising to die for Him.

- Thomas doubts that Jesus has actually risen from the dead.

God seems to accept—more easily than we Christians do—that humans are destined to live lives of moral failings and shortcomings. 'If God had real reservations about redeeming flawed humans, He would not have sent his Son to die on our behalf and we would be without a Savior. Fortunately, God is willing and able to forgive us.

In Texas we have a saying: "She's a hot mess." Let's accept the fact that each one of us is a hot mess. Once we admit it, we can receive God's grace through Jesus and be free.

God knows we'll fail, and He wants our humble repentance when we do. Even the most immoral person can choose to bow before God.

LEARNING ALERT

John's theme is that Jesus is on a mission to reveal—first to the Jews and then the Samaritans—that He is the Messiah (verse 26) and the Savior of the world (verse 42). Jesus loves the world, warts and all. This was a difficult message for Nicodemus and the Pharisees to accept. But the Samaritan woman got it and God used her to spread the word.

Lord, we are humble clay pots. We are not noble and righteous; we have no reason to feel proud. You have chosen to pour Your Spirit into humble and meek vessels who seem weak and frail from the outside. But on the inside, because of You, we carry the power, glory, and grace of the Almighty and Sovereign God of the universe. Help us to maintain our humility, but with gentle confidence may we realize and accept that we are forgiven, blessed and powerful vessels for Your grace and glory. Amen!

Discussion Questions

1. Of all the people you know, who is the last person you would expect God to use in His kingdom work? What about that person makes you think that way?

2. We are humble clay pots. What does that phrase mean to you? Does it better describe Nicodemus or the Samaritan woman?"

3. When has God used your words to impact others? Give an example or two.

LESSON 7
Could This Be the Christ?

John 4:27-42

> *[Jesus'] disciples came [to the well], and they were amazed that He had been speaking with a woman, yet no one said, "What do You seek?" or, "Why do You speak with her?" So the woman left her water pot and went into the city and said to the men, "Come, see a man who told me all the things that I have done; this is not the Christ, is it?" They went out of the city and were coming to Him....*
>
> *From that city, many of the Samaritans believed in Him because of the word of the woman who testified, "He told me all the things that I have done"... and they were saying to the woman, "It is no longer because of what you said that we believe, for we have heard for ourselves and know that this One is indeed the Savior of the world."*
> John 4:27-30, 38-42

Here in John 4, Jesus reveals that He is the Messiah for the Samaritans as well as the Jews. And clearly Christ's strategy for reaching the Samaritans is different than ours would be. In fact, it would seem to us that everything is wrong about what Jesus does here. If we wanted to impact Samaria, we'd seek out people of influence to spread the message. We'd go to the leading men of Samaria and convince them first. Our strategy would be that they, the leaders of Samaria, would then influence other Samaritans.

Jesus has a very different plan. You see, Jews don't normally talk to Samaritans. Jewish men do not initiate conversations with women, especially Samaritan women. Typically, a rabbi would instruct the men, and then the men would teach their wives and children. In this case, though, Jesus teaches the Samaritan woman, and then she *left her water pot, and went into the city and said to the* men..." (verse 28, emphasis added). She teaches the men—and she isn't even a very good teacher. She says, *"This is not the Christ, is it?"* (verse 29). Hardly a compelling sermon! Nevertheless, God uses her to spread the truth about Jesus. He uses her to reach an entire village.

And did you notice that all her friends and acquaintances seem to be men, not women? She is most likely an outcast among women because of her lifestyle. Samaritan women traveled to the well in groups; this woman is alone. Why do women despise her, and men befriend her? Rather obvious, I suppose. The point is, Jesus chooses a woman of tremendous moral failures.

Jesus reveals who He is to the most unlikely person imaginable. Nevertheless, verse 39 says, *From that city many of the Samaritans believed in Him because of the* word of the woman *who testified* (emphasis added).

LEARNING ALERT

Why do we allow our inadequacies to prevent us from being available to God? In the case of the Samaritan woman, the power of change for Samaria was the gospel message itself; the sinful messenger could not block that power. That's good because all of us are immensely inadequate, yet God can and does and will use us.

I recently turned 60 years old. Several weeks before my birthday, my bride sent out secret emails asking everyone I know to write me a note. Turning 60 prompts some to be reflective, as you might imagine. Add to that, getting dozens of notes from people whom I have been in contact with over many years gave me a lot more to think about. Reading those letters was very touching and emotional. Some of the most meaningful notes came from adults whom I'd ministered to 30 years ago when they were students and I was their youth pastor. Now they have teenagers themselves.

Another impactful aspect of these notes was the consistent mention of specific conversations or statements that I had influenced their lives. I don't remember most of the things I said. They weren't from speeches I'd made or carefully prepared sermons. The words God used were from normal conversations, and God used me to impact others. Just as He used the Samaritan woman. Let's just tell the truth—the gospel truth—and be kind. That's enough for God to work with!

Lord, help us. We feel like Isaiah might have…. When You called him to serve You, he responded, "Woe is me… because I am a man of unclean lips" (Isaiah 6:4). Those could be our words. We have unclean lips and hearts of flesh, and we are often overcome by our shortcomings and inadequacies. Lord, change our perspectives so that we will say every day and every hour, "Here I am. Send me!" just as Isaiah did (verse 8). Lord, You know that we are frail, weak, and sinful, but if You want to use us, we're ready and available. Amen!

Discussion Questions

1. Do you hesitate to enter ministry of some form because you don't qualify? If so, what does the story of the woman at the well say to you?

2. Why did the men listen to the woman?

3. What are some differences between insecurity and humility?

CHAPTER 5

THE WOMAN CAUGHT IN ADULTERY: SET FREE

LESSON 8
Caught in the Act

John 8:3-11

> The scribes and the Pharisees brought a woman caught in adultery and having set her in the center of the court, they said to Him, "Teacher, this woman has been caught in adultery, in the very act. Now in the Law, Moses commanded us to stone such women; what then do You say?" They were saying this, testing Him, so that they might have grounds for accusing Him. But Jesus stooped down and with His finger wrote on the ground....
>
> But when they persisted in asking Him, He straightened up, and said to them, "He who is without sin among you, let him be the first to throw a stone at her."
> John 8:3-7

This entire situation reeks of unfairness and injustice. In fact, it looks like a total setup.

Did you notice that no man is accused? According the Law of Moses, a man guilty of adultery is to be executed:

The adulterer and the adulteress shall surely be put to death.
Leviticus 10:10

If a man is found lying with a married woman, then both of them shall die, the man who lay with the woman, and the woman; thus, you shall purge the evil from Israel.
Deuteronomy 22:22

(I just thought I'd drop in some inspiring and devotional gems from our favorite devotional books of the Bible: Leviticus and Deuteronomy. Not Scripture you'd put to music, but these verses are part of the Law of Moses and were to be obeyed.)

Most likely, the man who had been with the woman was in on this plan to corner Jesus, and undoubtedly the Pharisees arranged the whole scenario in order to catch the woman and use her to trap Jesus.

THEY HAD HIM!

Jesus, the Friend of sinners, is caught in an apparent dilemma—just as the Pharisees planned. He has come not to *abolish* the Law but to *fulfill* it. So He has to agree with the sentence to condemn her to death because that's what God's

Law mandates. However, Jesus' circle of friends included tax collectors (mob bosses), prostitutes, thieves, and, now, adulterers. What will Jesus do? Will the Friend of sinners, the Lover of outcasts, and the Savior of the destitute follow the Law and endorse an execution?

LEARNING ALERT

How does God's perfect justice fit with His infinite mercy? Today's passage asks that question. We like to think that Jesus is the fullness of grace and mercy, and He is. But He is also fully God, and God is not only fully merciful, but fully just, as well. God is a consuming fire, and no sin will go unpunished. So what will Jesus' verdict be?

How will Jesus resolve this challenging issue? Will the perpetrators of this scheme get away with it? Have they caught Jesus in an irresolvable dilemma? A woman's life hangs in the balance. What will Jesus do?

Well, Jesus does what any rational person would do. He stoops down and writes in the dirt. Huh?

And people have wondered for centuries what Jesus wrote. Did He draw pictures, do a little doodling, or write out sentences? No one knows. The Greek word for "wrote" can describe drawing a figure as well as letters or words. I want to know!!! It's hard to accept simply not knowing.

So I'm going to speculate. I believe Jesus is writing something that paves the way for His spoken words to have a very strong impact. In silence, Jesus continues to write on the ground while the accusers persist in asking Jesus to answer. Finally, Jesus speaks: *"He who is without sin among you, let him be the first to throw a stone at her"* (John 8:7). More next time.

HOW, THEN, SHOULD WE LIVE?

As Christians, we know that we are not perfect and that we can't make ourselves perfect. But we are already perfect because of Jesus' sacrificial death on our behalf. Yet all of us continue to fall short. None of us is better than another. It is only by God's grace that we are forgiven and redeemed.

Lord, we are not to condemn fellow sinners, but how easily and often we fall into gossip, criticism, and slander? It feels good to point to someone who seems worse, or more sinful, than we are. This different focus takes the attention off us and falsely soothes our guilt.

But there's no place for superior airs or fake hierarchies among those of us who follow Jesus. When it comes to sin, we are all guilty. The woman was guilty, but so are we. All we have to cling to is Jesus and His forgivingness of our sins—and that is all we need.

Lord, help us not to condemn sinners. Instead, may we humbly pray for their hearts, that they would believe and receive You by faith. Amen!

Discussion Questions

1. Explain the balance of God's justice and His mercy in this world.

2. Is our role as human beings ever to condemn? To judge? Why or why not? Explain your answers.

3. What are some differences between how we believers respond to a sinning Christian and a sinning non-Christian?

LESSON 9
Sin No More

John 8:3-11

> *Straightening up, Jesus said to her, "Woman, where are they? Did no one condemn you?" She said, "No one, Lord." And Jesus said, "I do not condemn you, either. Go. From now on sin no more.*
> John 8:10-11

Let's go back to the accusers' statement that precedes Jesus' gentle and gracious words to the accused: *"He who is without sin among you, let him be the first to throw a stone at her"* (verse 7).

Now, this statement alone would strike the conscience of people who are aware of their own sins. What an effective reminder that we all are sinners! But the Pharisees' consciences are hardened, and they think of themselves as righteous and therefore worthy to judge and condemn. So— I'm speculating again!—I have to believe that what Jesus wrote on the ground somehow made public the accusers' personal sins. But we don't know for sure.

Here's the lesson Jesus is teaching: No one is worthy to judge and condemn this woman except Jesus Himself.

The words of Jesus and His writing on the ground clear the area. No one stays. Confronted by their own sins, they walk away from the Savior. Only the woman stays.

Why did she stay?

LEARNING ALERT

Whenever you come face to face with your sin, don't ever walk away from Jesus! Go toward your Savior! Don't run from Him. He will always forgive and accept the humble and contrite sinner. At this point in the narrative, we can learn from this woman.

Perhaps having nowhere to go, this woman stays at the feet of Jesus. She doesn't run away. She doesn't make excuses. She stays close to the Savior, knowing her only hope is in Him. The religious elite condemn her. But what will this Rabbi do?

Here are some significant points:

- When the Pharisees approach Jesus, they address Him as "teacher."

- The woman addresses Him as "Lord."

- When the Pharisees are confronted by Jesus, they walk away from the Savior.

- Caught in the act, the woman is guilty, burdened, and broken. So she stays with Jesus. In her heart, she must have said, "Lord, forgive me. I am a sinner."

Jesus deals with her heart and ours. We sin with our words and our actions. We can't be good enough to deserve or earn salvation. But praise God! Jesus deals with the heart. We are instructed to simply believe and receive. God doesn't expect us to be perfect.

Now, as promised in the previous lesson, I want to address a major theological issue that this story raises: How does God's perfect justice fit with His infinite mercy?

In that moment, all alone with the adulteress, Jesus does what only He can do: He is her judge, and He does not condemn her. Jesus extends His grace and His mercy.

LEARNING ALERT

After the Pharisees have wandered away and He is talking with the woman, Jesus is well aware of the full weight of the condemnation, pain, and terror He would soon endure on the cross for this woman's sin, for the sin of everyone who has ever and will ever walk this earth. Very shortly, He would be bearing the weight of her sin in His body on her behalf.

With His sacrificial death on the cross, Jesus will transfer to Himself the condemnation she deserves. I say this because I believe there is no other way for Jesus to say, "I do not condemn you." Jesus takes the condemnation off her and places it upon Himself. He bears her sin in His body. Justice is served, and mercy, love, grace, and forgiveness are extended.

Also, I don't believe that Jesus can make the statement "Go and sin no more," casually. Therefore, in her heart, on bended knee, in utter shame, with nowhere else to go, this woman must have believed and received Jesus as her Savior. Knowing both her heart and His imminent sacrifice that would cover her sin, Jesus declares, *"I do not condemn you"* (John 8:10). At that moment this woman joins the ranks of the forgiven! Now that she is saved, she is empowered by the Holy Spirit to walk away from her life of sin.

This is amazing—and beyond amazing! This is grace upon grace. This is forgiveness upon forgiveness.

And this is our Savior! The accusers couldn't trap Him between justice and grace. Why? Because He is the perfect fulfillment of *both*. Jesus fulfills both justice and grace, and He offers them to this precious, lovely woman who is filled with sin and facing a myriad of difficult issues. He extends perfect justice and complete grace and forgiveness to you as well by bearing your sin on Himself. What a Savior!

Jesus also extends perfect justice as well as complete grace and forgiveness to you and me. Each of us is a sinner with a trillion sins by our name; a sinner for whom Christ died; a sinner who is no longer condemned. That is the staggering truth of Romans 8:1—*There is now no condemnation for those who are in Christ Jesus.*

Jesus, You fulfill both justice and grace for us. May we never leave You. May we stay with You even if everyone else departs. Hear the prayers of our heart. Lord, I receive Your forgiveness and accept You by faith. We will be forever grateful that You endured judgment because of our sin. We will be forever grateful for Your grace and mercy. Amen!

Discussion Questions

1. Do you sometimes feel condemned by other Christians? Is that a them-issue or a you-issue? Explain.

2. Does not condemning someone mean we let people we care about go on sinning without saying anything? Explain the differences.

3. When, if ever, have you run from Jesus? Why? What were the results of your choice?

4. Describe in your own words how God's perfect justice and unfailing grace work together rather than cancel each other out.

CHAPTER 6

MARY AND MARTHA:

FAITH UNLEASHED

LESSON 10
Jesus' Discipleship Classroom

John 11:1-44

> Now a certain man was sick, Lazarus of Bethany, the village of Mary and her sister Martha...So the sisters sent word to Him saying, "Lord, behold, he whom you love is sick." But when Jesus heard this, He said, "This sickness is not to end in death, but for the glory of God, so that the Son of God may be glorified by it." Now Jesus loved Martha and her sister and Lazarus.
>
> Therefore, when Mary came where Jesus was, she saw Him and fell at His feet, saying to Him, "Lord, if You had been here, my brother would not have died." When Jesus therefore saw her weeping, ... He was deeply moved in spirit and was troubled, and said, "Where have you laid him?" They said to Him. "Lord, come and see." Jesus wept.
> John 11:1, 3-5, 32-35

John 11 is the account of Jesus raising Lazarus from the dead. In my reading and reflecting, I saw two primary observations and lessons. First is a lesson on the extent of a believer's faith and trust, and second is a beautiful picture of the tender compassion of Jesus has for those He loves.

This passage is timely for me today because I sometimes struggle with doubt and uncertainty about the future. This fact humbles me because I usually view myself as strong in faith and able to stand firm in God's sovereignty. Nevertheless, I've let anxiety creep into my soul.

John 11 tells of two women of faith, believers who love Jesus and whom Jesus loves. The sisters love Jesus and have great faith in Him, but in the case of their brother's illness, Jesus challenges the extent of their faith. I can relate.

The narrative makes it clear that Jesus loves these three siblings:

- Verse 5 says, "Jesus loved *Martha, her sister and Lazarus.*"

- Verse 11, Jesus says, "Our friend *Lazarus has fallen asleep.*"

- Verse 33-34 says, "*When Jesus therefore saw her weeping...*He was deeply moved *in spirit and* was troubled."

- *Jesus* wept (verse 35).

I'll come back to the tender heart that Jesus has for these much-loved followers. But let's get back to the flow of the narrative.

Jesus hears that Lazarus is sick. In most cases, when we hear that a loved one is sick to the point of death, we would move quickly to be at their side. But Jesus pauses, and He has some very specific reasons for doing so. Jesus intentionally delays going to Lazarus so that He might glorify Himself and build up the faith of His disciples. His followers need another important lesson before Jesus goes away. After all, the cross is just a few days away, and the disciples are going to be tested far beyond any test they've experienced thus far.

You see, Jesus has shown His followers His courage, boldness, and intellect when He cleansed the temple and confronted and confounded the Pharisees. He has also performed such miracles as turning water into wine, walking on water, multiplying food, and healing some who had been plagued with lifelong illnesses. The disciples had a front-row view of the power and deity of Jesus. All of this has been Jesus preparing them for life as a Christian leader, a calling that would bring massive opposition and ultimate martyrdom.

As a result of Jesus' mentorship, the disciples have a certain measure of faith and hope in Him. They already have a myriad of lessons to reflect on after Jesus is gone, but the lessons aren't complete yet. The disciples need more. They aren't yet ready to maintain their faith when they see their Messiah nailed to a cross, pronounced dead, and buried. Jesus is going to use Mary and Martha's real-life experience to teach the disciples a new lesson. At the same time, we are going to see Jesus' tender heart of love for these amazing women.

LEARNING ALERT

This miracle of Lazarus is a climatic event in the life of Jesus' followers, a miracle that they don't yet fully comprehend. The disciples need this lesson on the power of God to raise a person from the dead in order to be ready to face Jesus's death with some faith. Jesus tells the disciples, *"Lazarus is dead, and I am glad for your sakes that I was not there [to heal his sickness], so that you may believe" [more than you do now]"* (verses 14-15).

Jesus will also strengthen the faith of Mary and Martha who already have a solid faith in Jesus. Because of His tender love and care for them, He wants them to be prepared for facing His death on the cross. (We'll look at the faith of Mary and Martha in the next lesson.)

Jesus' discipleship classroom is a rigorous place. Many days I'd often prefer to skip school! You see, at this prep school for aspiring disciples, Jesus doesn't always let us know what the lesson plan is for each day. Sometimes the lesson is a glorious, inspirational blessing of wondrous insights into the glory of God. On other days the lessons involve trials, difficulties, and sorrow.

The discipleship lessons that Jesus teaches us when a loved one dies are especially hard—and we'll see in our next lesson that Jesus doesn't enjoy teaching this lesson. Nevertheless, He does it because death is an extraordinary learning opportunity. Mary and Martha are sad and even angry that Jesus has only now arrived. They are very reluctant students for any lesson that their beloved brother's death offers. You've probably been angry and frustrated with God when a loved one died. It is a painful, painful time.

Have you learned what Jesus wants to teach you from the loss of your loved one? If you're still too angry to learn, that's OK. God will stay close to you and will comfort you as needed. And regardless of how long ago the death was, when you're ready, He will also teach you a greater lesson on strength, courage, and faith. It's a lesson we can't learn anywhere else because nothing compares to losing a loved one to death. When you're ready, He's ready to help you through it and lead you to a new level of faith.

HOW, THEN, SHOULD WE LIVE?

Is there anything our God can't do? Jesus, we are so much like Your disciples. Our faith is often limited to what we have seen or tied up in our emotions. Like Mary and Martha, we make our "if" and "but" statements that reveal our limited faith. But, Jesus, You replied, "Did I not say to you that if you believe, you will see the glory of God?" (verse 40). Lord, I say that I'm a firm believer in Your power and Your sovereignty, but I ask that You take this belief beyond my lips and set it deep in my heart. Amen!

Discussion Questions

1. Is your faith limited to what you have seen? If so, is that really faith? Why or why not? And if you answered no, explain and perhaps give an example.

2. What are some ways you can expand your faith?

3. In what ways does the fact that we have nothing to fear, not even death, affect the way you live? Be specific.

WHAT I'VE LEARNED FROM AMAZING WOMEN OF THE BIBLE

LESSON 11
Lazarus Lives Again

John 11:1-44

> *Therefore, when Mary came where Jesus was, she saw*
> *Him, and fell at His feet, saying to Him, "Lord, if You had*
> *been here, my brother would not have died." When Jesus*
> *therefore saw her weeping... He was deeply moved in*
> *spirit and was troubled, and said, "Where have you laid*
> *him?" They said to Him. "Lord, come and see." Jesus wept.*
> John 11:20-21, 32-35

Mary and Martha are true believers, and this passage affirms their tremendous faith. They believe that Jesus, their Lord, has the power to heal. He has done it before. So the nagging question in their minds is *Why hadn't He come earlier and healed their beloved brother Lazarus, before he died?*

Yes, the sisters have faith, but their statements reveal the extent of their faith: they did not yet know all that Jesus could do. In simple terms, Mary and Martha believe that Jesus can *heal,* but they don't know that He can also *raise* from the dead. Quite frankly, who can really blame them? Jesus' power is beyond their comprehension. And ours as well.

Later, the believers who are mourning with Mary and Martha, ask, *"Could not this man, who opened the eyes of the blind man, have kept this man also from dying?"* (verse 37). We have a theme here, folks! The miracles performed so far took these believers' faith to a certain point. But raising a man from the dead after decomposition has begun??? Well, that calls for a new level of faith—and that is the point of Jesus' plan. He wants to take their faith to a whole new level so they are better prepared for the pressing need for faith that is to come.

> Jesus said to [Martha], "Did I not say to you that if you believe, you will see the glory of God?" ... When He had said these things, He cried out with a loud voice, "Lazarus, come forth." The man who had died came forth, bound hand and foot with wrappings, and his face was wrapped around with a cloth. Jesus said to them, "Unbind him, and let him go."
> John 11: 40, 43-44

In a matter of days, the disciples will see Jesus crucified. How crucial for Jesus to show them that death does not hold Him! Death does not constrain Him. Jesus *is* the Resurrection and the Life. How kind of Jesus to reveal to them His power over death and thereby strengthen their faith for the dark days of His betrayal and crucifixion.

And that brings me to the other lesson from this narrative.

TENDER LOVE

In this account of Lazarus being raised from the dead, we clearly see Jesus' tender love for His followers. Sometimes Jesus takes us through difficult trials in order to teach us and strengthen our faith. These trials are never easy, but Jesus knows how we are wired. Difficulties can and do strengthen our faith and increase our dependency on Him. Tough times build our faith.

But how does Jesus feel about taking us through difficult trials? Is it easy for Him? We have a view into His heart from His interaction with Mary.

> *When Jesus therefore saw her weeping... He was deeply moved in spirit and was troubled, and said, "Where have you laid him?" They said to Him, "Lord, come and see." Jesus wept.*
> (verses 33-35)

Previously I never fully understood why Jesus weeps. It wouldn't be over Lazarus dying because Jesus knows He is going to raise him from the dead. So why does He weep? It's now so clear to me. I just needed to read the verse in context.

LEARNING ALERT

In order to teach His disciples, Mary and Martha that He is sovereign over death, Jesus chooses to allow Lazarus to die. However, the death of Lazarus causes tremendous emotional pain for his loving sisters. When Jesus arrives at the siblings' house, Mary falls to His feet and weeps. She is heartbroken and deeply distressed. Her mourning is profound. And because of His love for her, Jesus feels her pain as if it is His own. Even though He knows she will be happy again very soon, it pains Him to put her through this experience.

He weeps because she weeps. He is troubled because she is troubled. Out of tender love and empathy, Jesus weeps.

If Jesus takes you through trials in order to strengthen you, He doesn't do it without deeply feeling your pain. Just because He takes us through hardship doesn't mean He enjoys it. He weeps alongside us.

What a Savior You are! What tender love and empathy You have for us! Jesus, we can't thank You enough for Your compassion and Your presence with us during our trials. It pains You to take us through them, but You know that they produce good in our character and grow our faith. You know that hard times strengthen us and teach us to persevere in our daily walk with You. We don't always understand why events unfold as they do, but we choose—by faith—to trust in You. Amen!

Discussion Questions

1. Why do you think Jesus wept?

2. Was it good that Lazarus died? Why or why not?

3. In what ways does God show His power in your life? Could He do more? Explain your answer to the second question.

4. What insight into your death and resurrection does the account of Lazarus provide you?

LESSON 12
Sisters

Luke 10:38-42 and John 11:33-36

About to enter the last week of His earthly life, Jesus returns to Bethany and the home of Lazarus and his sisters, Mary and Martha. During His three years of itinerant preaching and healing, this house seems to be where Jesus is most comfortable.

In John 12, as Jesus nears the moment of the Triumphal Entry, John paints the contrast between love and hate, between devotion and contempt. First the love and devotion.

SERVING OR SITTING?

I'm sure Martha and Mary love each other, but I suspect they also drive each other a little crazy from time to time. Martha has all the tendencies of the firstborn, maternal sister. She is more grown up, responsible, organized, and hardworking. In contrast, Mary is flighty, creative, and emotional. She seems a real romantic who might have fairy-tale dreams and a vivid imagination.

Sure, I'm speculating, but after reading the Bible's three stories about Martha and Mary, I think I'm pretty close. Luke 10:38-42, for instance, tells about what happened over supper when Jesus was in their home.

[Jesus] entered a village, and a woman named Martha welcomed Him into her home. She had a sister called

Mary, who was seated at the Lord's feet, listening to His word. But Martha was distracted with all her preparations; and she came up to Him and said, "Lord, do You not care that my sister has left me to do all the serving alone? Then tell her to help me." But the Lord answered and said to her, "Martha, Martha, you are worried and bothered about so many things; but only one thing is necessary, for Mary has chosen the good part, which shall not be taken away from her."
Luke 10:38-42

I feel bad for Martha. Jesus is pretty blunt with her. Hopefully, Mary isn't one to rub it in Martha's face. But even if she doesn't, Martha feels bad enough. She has felt the force of Jesus' commendation of Mary's actions over hers. Sisters!

GRIEVING—AND ACCUSING

Second is the account of Lazarus's death. Jesus delays coming to them, and when He finally arrives, Lazarus has been dead for four days. When Martha and Mary hear that Jesus is near, Mary stays at the house, and Martha goes out to meet Him. Why did the loving and worshipful Mary stay behind? Again, I'm speculating, but I believe Mary is overcome with grief and perhaps is even mad at Jesus for His delay. Jesus took His time getting there, and now Lazarus is dead! Mary knows that Jesus could have healed her brother if He'd hustled to get there. So Martha goes out to Jesus and has a conversation with Him. I'm sure she is emotional, but there's no mention of tears. As they talk, Martha asserts her belief that Jesus is the Christ and declares her faith that He can and will raise her brother—in the final resurrection. She doesn't yet realize the extent of the miracle Jesus is about to perform.

Martha gets back to the house, assumes the maternal role, and tells Mary that she needs to go see Jesus. Martha wants Mary to do the right thing. That's how Martha is wired. Sisters!

Mary runs to Jesus, falls at His feet, and weeps uncontrollably. In her emotional state, she begins to lecture Jesus that if He had been there, He could have saved her brother. Jesus is so moved by her weeping and deep emotional pain that He begins to weep Himself.

> *When Mary came where Jesus was, she saw Him, and fell at His feet, saying to Him, "Lord, if You had been here, my brother would not have died." When Jesus saw her weeping, and the Jews who came with her also weeping, He was deeply moved in spirit and was troubled ... Jesus wept.*
> John 11:33-34, 36

LEARNING ALERT

Both sisters believe in Jesus! They call Him "Lord," and they affirm their belief that He is the Christ and the Son of God. They are both devoted to Jesus, but they express their devotion differently. Jesus tells Martha she can learn from Mary, but that didn't mean she should be like Mary. Sisters!

Remembering this backdrop, we'll look at the third story of Jesus in the home of Martha and Mary next time.

Lord, throughout Your Word, You call us to live out both love and truth. Our relationship with You is from the heart and the mind. Martha is more rational, and Mary is more emotional. We are to worship in spirit and in truth. Help us to devote time to developing our mind with Your truth and time to worship You with our heart, soul, and emotions. Help us also to be patient with believers who worship Jesus differently than we do. Rather than critique them, may we learn from them, and may we grow in the grace and knowledge of You. Amen!

LARRY SHAFFER

Discussion Questions

1. Do you have a sibling whom you try—or have tried—to change? Do you have a sibling who tries—or has tried—to change you? Comment on the dynamics in both situations. What are some of the results of these efforts?

2. Do you feel the author's speculations about Mary and Martha are correct? Why or why not?

3. Why is diversity in the church a good thing? Give several reasons.

LESSON 13
A Valuable Lesson

John 12:1-12

> *Jesus, therefore, six days before the Passover, came to Bethany where Lazarus was, whom Jesus had raised from the dead. So, they made Him a supper there, and Martha was serving; but Lazarus was one of those reclining at the table with Him. Mary then took a pound of very costly perfume of pure nard and anointed the feet of Jesus and wiped His feet with her hair; and the house was filled with the fragrance of the perfume.*
> John 12:1-3

It's suppertime at the home of Lazarus and his sisters, Martha and Mary. Once again, Martha is preparing and serving. As is the custom, the men are reclined at the table. Lazarus, whom Jesus loves, is with Jesus. Martha is serving and most likely doesn't even bother to ask Mary for help anymore. Mary is a free spirit. She is overwhelmed with joy. Her beloved brother is alive. Her Lord and Savior is in the house. What a celebration!

Mary is being Mary: sitting at the feet of Jesus, listening to His every word, seeming oblivious to the physical needs of serving dinner. Then, in an act of worship and devotion, Mary takes one of her most prized possessions—expensive perfume—and pours it on Jesus' feet. Huge gasp!

According to the text, the cost of this bottle of perfume is 300 denarii. In today's currency, that would be about

$50,000. To Mary, the cost of the perfume is absolutely irrelevant. Its high value reveals her devotion to Jesus. To me—and probably to Martha—that's just crazy.

My wife, Leigh, is like Mary, and she doesn't appreciate it when I limit her giving heart. I have certain criteria and principles of giving that I prefer to follow. I'm a warm-hearted rationalist.

On the other hand, she sees a need and wants to give—and, in most cases, give a lot. I've learned a lot from her in the area of giving, and she humbly listens to my reasoning. Together, we strike a pretty good balance, but if Jesus were in my house, He would most likely whisper in my ear, "Don't hold back her heart. Let her give."

But back to Mary and her act of pure love and devotion. It seems she doesn't have a rational bone in her body. I suspect she doesn't evaluate all the facts and consider the pros and cons before she breaks the bottle of perfume. No, she just acted.

The warm-hearted rationalist—me!—has some questions. Wouldn't just a few drops of the expensive perfume do the job? Couldn't she wait until after supper so that the pervasive odor doesn't wreck the meal that Martha is working so hard to prepare? What about the shock Lazarus may experience when he sees what his sister is doing? After all, Lazarus's hard work may have been the only reason Mary even has that perfume! Also at dinner is Judas, who condemns the act and self-righteously states that the perfume would be better used if it were sold and the money was used to feed the poor.

LEARNING ALERT

As far we can tell, none of the bystanders consider Mary's act either reasonable or commendable. Almost none. One Person there loves Mary's act of heartfelt worship. Jesus commends her and also indicates that the act is prophetic, representing preparation for His burial.

> Jesus said, "Let her alone, so that she may keep it for the day of My burial. For you always have the poor with you, but you do not always have Me.'" (verse 7)

Lord, help us be more like Mary, a lover and worshipper of Jesus. May we worship from our heart with passion and joy. May we not cling to money and possessions; may we not view them as ours. All we have is Yours. All we are is Yours. So, by faith, we release all that we are and all that we have for You to use for Your glory. You alone are worthy of all praise. Amen!

Discussion Questions

1. Should Martha be more like Mary? Or should Mary be more like Martha? Why or why not?

2. Do you get uncomfortable when people show too much emotion in worship? Why or why not?

3. Are you more rational or more emotional? Describe how the way you're wired affects your worship.

CHAPTER 7

RUTH: REDEEMED!

LESSON 14
You're Beautiful!

Psalm 149:4

> *The Lord takes pleasure in His people;*
>
> *He will beautify the afflicted ones with salvation.*
> Psalm 149:4

SOME BASICS

The book of Ruth is a gem tucked away in the Old Testament. Here are a few key principles that are helpful whenever you explore an Old Testament book:

1. The essence of the Old Testament is the persevering love of a faithful God who will fulfill His covenants. In Eden He promised that the seed of Eve will eventually lead to the birth of the Messiah, who will destroy Satan. God promises to Abraham the

expansion of the Israelite nation, to the ultimate fulfillment of promises like these in the birth of Jesus, our Messiah. Nothing will stop God from His plan to send a Savior first as the sacrificial Lamb, and second, as a roaring, victorious Lion of Judah.

2. The thread of the Messiah's coming and our future redemption is woven into each Old Testament book. It is especially evident in the book of Ruth.

3. Old Testament books emphasize certain attributes of God. Be on the lookout for which of God's characteristics shine brightly in the book of Ruth.

The epic love story found in the book of Ruth will leave us wondering at the goodness and faithfulness of God!

GOD AT WORK

I discovered Psalm 149:4 one morning as I was randomly doing some cross referencing for another study. When I read this verse, I realized that it describes the theme of Ruth beautifully:

The Lord takes pleasure in His people;

He will beautify the afflicted ones with salvation.

To beautify means "to clothe; to remove ragged, soiled garments and dress with the wardrobe of royalty." Psalm 149:4 describes the Lord's work in Ruth's, as well as in my life and yours. The Lord will fulfill His covenant promises by beautifying *the afflicted ones with salvation.*

GOD'S WAY

One might think that, in fulfilling the Abrahamic Covenant, God would be concerned about keeping pure the bloodline from Abraham to Jesus. In the succession of human royalty, a pure bloodline is important.

The Old Testament reveals that God does, in fact, keep the bloodline pure but not in the usual manner. In the book of Ruth, we will see God insert into Jesus' family tree an Amorite harlot, a son of a harlot, and an idol-worshipping widow from the nation of Moab, a nation that resulted from an act of incest. Their bloodline was corrupt from Day One!

And God inserts these corrupt people into the Messianic bloodline without corrupting it by *beautifying the afflicted with the garments of salvation.* God takes the impure and makes them pure. He replaces filthy rags with robes of royalty. He transforms the poor and afflicted into the spiritually rich and famous. He makes the ignoble noble. He makes the children of incest the holy children of God and He makes the harlot pure and clean.

LEARNING ALERT

God does for you and me what He did for His people Israel and the Messianic line. God redeems us sinners with His righteousness. He did this for Ruth, and by God's grace,

He will redeem you as well when you put your faith in Jesus. That's the Good News for us—and for us to share with our friends, family, neighbors, and co-workers.

Lord, thank You for making me pure, holy and noble in Your sight, through the grace of Jesus. Amen!

Discussion Questions

1. How does God see you? Clean? Pure? Noble? Explain why you answered as you did.

2. Maybe you just touched on this, but why does God see you the way He does?

3. Why does God have this different perspective?

LESSON 15
An Epic Love Story

The book of Ruth is an epic love story that showcases kindness, grace, and virtue. The events take place during the time of the judges and a couple generations before David.

THE FOREIGNER

In a word, the story is heartwarming in the end. The Old Testament has plenty of tragedy and wickedness, but Ruth's almost fairy-tale story has a heartwarming conclusion. Enjoy reading this account of noble, virtuous, and God-fearing people who endure difficulties and are blessed by God with a happy ending.

The main characters are Naomi, Ruth, and Boaz. The widow Naomi is Ruth's mother-in-law, the widow Ruth is a Moabite, and Boaz is a relative of Naomi's late husband. As the story unfolds, these themes emerge:

1. *The character of a godly woman:* Although Ruth is both a foreigner and a convert to the God of Israel, Ruth has a reputation as a *woman of excellence* (Ruth 3:11).

2. *Blessings on a foreigner:* The picture of God so fully blessing a foreigner foreshadows our present situation as Gentiles. Through Christ, God has extended His grace beyond Israel to Gentiles as well as, in Ruth's case, Moabites.

3. *Despair before joy:* The heartwarming comes after a period of despair. The circumstances are volatile, but the character of the godly people in this story is stable and consistent.

4. *Redemption:* Throughout the story we see God's redemptive plan for Ruth coming together. Boaz, her redeemer, foreshadows Jesus who is our Redeemer.

FLYING THROUGH THE CLOUDS

Perhaps you've been on a flight and found the plane in zero visibility. You looked out the window and could see absolutely nothing. That in itself was a little unnerving, but then came the turbulence. Things were getting bounced around in the cabin as the flight attendant announced that you were on final descent.

As you continued to look out the window, you strained to see land… and couldn't.

Then the pilot came on. In a calm and reassuring voice, he said, "Ladies and gentlemen, this is Captain Wright from the flight deck. We certainly want to thank you for flying with us today. As you can tell, we've encountered some clouds. We'll get under the cloud bank in a couple of minutes, and then you'll see a beautiful New England day. Thanks again for flying with us."

That's all it took. With words from the pilot, your anxiety went away. You weren't as frantic to see land when you looked out the window, and you loosened your grip on the armrest. Why? There was still no sight of land. There was still turbulence and the direction of the plane was still downward.

What had changed? The pilot had told you good weather was ahead. He knew things you couldn't know, and he assured you that all was well.

I'm sure you see the parallels. Circumstances in life are grim. Problems rain down. Stress sets in. Then we hear the voice of our Father. Able to see things we can't see; He assures us that everything's going to be OK.

We can relax and breathe. We can trust that He knows what He's talking about. But up ahead, there is beautiful weather. It's going to be great!

That's good news!

LEARNING ALERT

As we unpack this story, let's ask God to reveal how we should live.

Lord, our lives are challenging, but Your steady hand and Your commitment to fulfill Your plan offer stability. May You build our faith as we study the book of Ruth and consider her steady example, *the example of Ruth, a woman of excellence. Amen!*

Discussion Questions

1. In looking back over your life, when did a blessing come after dire circumstances or despair? What was darkness? What was the blessing? What lesson(s) did you learn?

2. Which of the four themes of Ruth (identified above) do you feel will be most relevant to you? Why?

3. Is it fair that the Israelites are God's chosen people, yet Gentiles can get the same blessings of salvation and redemption? Explain your answer.

LESSON 16
Down, But Not Out

Ruth

I've learned that my devotions are richer when I take the time to do some basic research. I find it helpful to learn how the particular book fits into biblical history and how the themes fit into the biblical story. So I've learned, for instance, that the book of Ruth was written shortly before, or early into King David's reign. Also, lineage was important to the Jews, and Ruth 4:16-22 establishes that Ruth is David's great-grandmother. Also, Ruth is one of only four women mentioned in Matthew's genealogy of Jesus.

SEEMINGLY UNIMPORTANT

Ruth is a very special woman. Despite the male-dominated culture of her time, Ruth emerges as a woman of significant influence. She displays character and integrity at the highest level. She clothes herself in virtue, loyalty, and kindness. As such, she teaches us the powerful lesson that "seemingly unimportant people appear at apparently insignificant times which later prove to be monumentally crucial to accomplishing God's will" (*The MacArthur Study Bible, Thomas Nelson 2013*).

THANKS A LOT

Ruth was a Moabite. When she goes to her mother-in-law's homeland of Israel, that Moabite heritage isn't just a strike against Ruth, it's almost unforgivable. You see, Abraham's nephew Lot fathered Moab by an incestuous act with his oldest daughter. So the Moabite nation has long been an enemy of God's people. Israelites despise Moabites.

Consider Ruth's plight. She doesn't have much going for her:

1. She is a Moabite.

2. 2. After her young husband dies, Ruth follows her mother-in-law, Naomi, to Bethlehem and lives in humble means as a maidservant. She is essentially a beggar.

3. 3. Ruth is a female in a male-dominated society.

Despite these strikes against her, Ruth ultimately marries a wealthy and prominent man. In fact, she becomes the great-grandmother of King David and, farther down the line, an ancestor of Jesus Himself. Wow! Not bad for a foreigner!

WHAT CAN WE LEARN FROM RUTH?

Ruth achieves greatness and significance, but not because she pursues it. God doesn't ask us to pursue greatness and significance. Instead, He expects us to receive Him by faith and then to walk humbly and obediently with Him throughout our days.

You see, on any given day and in seemingly routine events, God can and will use us for His purposes. We do well, then, to approach each day with a humble commitment to virtue, loyalty, and kindness. As we go through the day, God will—if we ask Him—help us make moment-by-moment decisions that align with His principles. Who knows what God may do in and around you! When you stumble—and we all stumble—get back up, ask God for forgiveness, recommit yourself to honoring Him with your life and keep going.

Father, guide us to live as we see in the example of Ruth with simplicity and sincerity of devotion to our God. Build within us a foundation of discipline that we might live out the calling from the prophet Micah, 'to do justice, to love kindness and to walk humbly with our God.' Amen.

Discussion Questions

1. What obstacles to walking humbly and obediently with God have you encountered?

2. What have you done to try to overcome those obstacles? What actions have been most effective?

3. Ruth definitely has some strikes against her. What strikes do you feel you have against you? What have you done—what are you doing—to deal with them effectively?

LESSON 17
No Place to Turn

Ruth 1:1-9

> *Now it came about in the days when the judges governed,*
> *that there was a famine in the land. And a certain*
> *man of Bethlehem in Judah went to sojourn in the land*
> *of Moab with his wife and his two sons. The name of the*
> *man was Elimelech, and the name of his wife, Naomi;*
> *and the names of his two sons were Mahlon and Chilion,*
> *Ephrathites of Bethlehem in Judah. Now they entered*
> *the land of Moab and remained there. Then Elimelech,*
> *Naomi's husband, died; and she was left with her two*
> *sons. They took for themselves Moabite women as wives;*
> *the name of the one was Orpah and the name of the other*
> *Ruth. And they lived there about ten years. Then both*
> *Mahlon and Chilion also died, and the woman was*
> *bereft of her two children and her husband.*
>
> *Then she arose with her daughters-in-law that she*
> *might return from the land of Moab, for she had heard*
> *in the land of Moab that the LORD had visited His*
> *people in giving them food. So she departed from the*
> *place where she was, and her two daughters-in-law with*
> *her; and they went on the way to return to the land of*
> *Judah. And Naomi said to her two daughters-in-law,*
> *"Go, return each of you to her mother's house. May*
> *the LORD deal kindly with you as you have dealt with*
> *the dead and with me. May the LORD grant that you*

may find rest, each in the house of her husband. Then
she kissed them, and they lifted up their voices and wept.
Ruth 1:1-9

The story begins during the time of the judges, a couple
of generations before David arrives on the scene. When a
famine hits Judah, a man named Elimelech from Bethlehem
makes the difficult decision to escape the famine and move
his wife, Naomi, and their two sons to the foreign land
of Moab. Shortly after arriving in Moab, Elimelech dies.
Despite this tragedy, life of course goes on. In time, the two
sons marry Moabite women, Orpah (not Oprah!) and Ruth.
After living in Moab for 10 years, both sons die. Maybe the
whole Moab decision was a mistake???

Early in our marriage, I decided to move my wife, Leigh,
from her hometown in Florida, all the way across the country,
to my hometown of Seattle, Washington. I was driven to
advance my career as a youth minister, and I made her lots
of promises about how wonderful the whole situation would
be. Of course Leigh was nervous, but she agreed, and off
we went on a new adventure. Oh yeah, I almost forgot to
mention that Leigh had just turned 22 years old and was
four months pregnant with our first child.

To make a long story short, nothing in Seattle worked
out well. I was frustrated at work, and things were volatile
on the home front. I love that city, but one of the challenging
realities was... the weather. We moved in February and
didn't see a sunny day until June. For a 22-year-old pregnant

girl from Florida, that was tough—and it was difficult for me as well. We both vividly remember the lack of sunshine for the first 5 months we lived there—and the glorious way that period ended. Our daughter was born on June 23, and that was the first blue-skied, sunny day of our residence together in Seattle. Then, 12 months after Leigh gave birth, we moved back to the Southeast United States.

Looking back, I'm confident that leaving Florida was the right decision. But was the whole 18-month adventure to Seattle a mistake? We now know that it was an important part of our journey as a husband and wife. That season was very important in God's plan to strip me of pride and selfishness. More on that later.

THE BONDS OF LOVE AND DEVOTION

Back to the biblical story. I'm curious how the father and sons die, but there's no hint. I guess that information isn't relevant to God's story and why He's telling it. What *is* relevant, however, is that Naomi—broken-hearted and left alone without any men in her life to bring in some income— decides to go home to Bethlehem.

Apparently a godly woman, kind and gracious, Naomi tells her daughters-in-law to return to their parents' homes:

> *"Go, return each of you to her mother's house. May the LORD deal kindly with you as you have dealt kindly with the dead and with me. May the LORD grant that you find*

> *rest, each in the house of her husband.". Then she kissed*
> *them, and they lifted up their voices and wept.*
> Ruth 1:8-10

Clearly, these women share a genuine bond of love and devotion forged during the 10 years they have lived life together.

I can only assume that Naomi is a wonderful, godly mentor to these young girls, encouraging them to love the God of Israel whom she loves. We will see that Naomi's influence of Ruth is indeed significant and life changing. In fact, Naomi's influence over Ruth also influenced history. But to our point here, despite her emotional pain, Naomi remains a positive and godly influence on these two daughters-in-law. *We never know how much God might use us—or be using us—in the lives of others.*

LET'S BE INTENTIONAL

Our words, our actions, our prayers for others--all of these contribute to the impact we have on those we meet and interact with. Please consider people you can influence and then determine—with God's help—whether you will be intentional as a mentor or an unintentional influence.

Being intentional takes our praying and planning to a higher level. Now we are able to take certain actions, allocate time, and truly invest in the person(s) we hope to mentor. Prayerfully consider this calling today—and may the Lord grant you His grace and love to be positive influences on all with whom you come in contact today.

LEARNING ALERT

It occurs to me that when you and I are willing to yield to God, God can use us to influence others just as He used Naomi in Ruth's life.

Lord, please make us mindful of Your power in us to positively impact others. Please give us eyes to see opportunities to help others and the faith to trust that You can work through even our simple actions. Amen!

Discussion Questions

1. Are you aware of people who have been intentional about impacting you with God's love through small but consistent kindnesses? List some of their actions and determine the best way you might thank them.

2. Who has been intentional about influencing you regarding your faith? Note what that person did/does and some of the ways you benefited.

3. Who has God placed on your heart to disciple and mentor?

LESSON 18
Determined

Ruth 1:11-19

Naomi said, "Return, my daughters. Why should you go with me? Have I yet sons in my womb, that they may be your husbands? Return, my daughters! Go, for I am too old to have a husband. If I said I have hope, if I should even have a husband tonight and also bear sons, would you therefore wait until they were grown? Would you therefore refrain from marrying? No, my daughters; for it is harder for me than for you, for the hand of the LORD has gone forth against me."

And they lifted up their voices and wept again; and Orpah kissed her mother-in-law, but Ruth clung to her.

Then she said, "Behold, your sister-in-law has gone back to her people and her gods; return after your sister-in-law." But Ruth said, "Do not urge me to leave you or turn back from following you; for where you go, I will go, and where you lodge, I will lodge. Your people shall be my people, and your God, my God. Where you die, I will die, and there I will be buried. Thus may the LORD do to me, and worse, if anything but death parts you and me." When she saw that she was determined to go with her, she said no more to her.

So they both went until they came to Bethlehem. And when they had come to Bethlehem, all the city was stirred because of them, and women said, "Is this Naomi?"
Ruth 1:11-19

After the death of her husband and two sons in Moab, Naomi determines to go home to Bethlehem. The famine in Judah has ended, and she has no reason to stay in Moab. She encourages her daughters-in-law to remain in their homeland. After all, Naomi explains, she is old and has no sons for them to marry. She urges them to go home, find a husband, and make a life for themselves, *"for the hand of the LORD has gone forth against me"* (verse 13). Orpah weeps, kisses Naomi, and departs, but Ruth clings to her mother-in-law and will not leave.

YOUR GOD, MY GOD

With love and affection, Naomi says to Ruth, *"Behold, your sister-in-law has gone back to her people and her gods; return after your sister-in-law."* Then Ruth responds with one of the book's key verses. Ruth's words reveal not only Ruth's devotion to Naomi, but also her heart's conversion to the true God of Israel and her unwillingness to return to the Moabite gods.

Ruth says, *"Do not urge me to leave you or turn back from following you; for where you go, I will go, and where you lodge, I will lodge.* Your people shall be my people; and your God, my God"* (Ruth 1:16, emphasis added).

Orpah and Ruth have spent 10 years with this Jewish family. Orpah, I'm sure, followed the rules of the house and participated in the Jewish rituals. She was a faithful wife to Naomi's son. But when the opportunity presents itself—and when it appears that the God of Israel is against Naomi—Orpah goes back to her family and their gods.

Ruth, on the other hand, reveals her heart transformation and new devotion to the God of Israel. The rituals of Judaism are not just rituals to Ruth. They have become a true expression of Ruth's heart. She isn't willing to leave her spiritual mentor or forsake her God, the true God of Israel. Even though it appears that the God of Israel is against Naomi, Ruth knows by faith that God is true and faithful. Her devotion to God and to Naomi is firm, faithful, and enduring.

TRUE FAITH

We can learn much from Ruth. First, she knows by faith that the current dire circumstances are *not* an indication that God is against them even though her mentor says as much. Ruth's faith is true, fortified in the fire of loss and uncertainty about their future. Have you ever been there?

Ruth has nothing. No money to fall back on. No security of any kind. As some would say, the sky was falling. Yet Ruth decides to stay the course. She will remain with her mother-in-law and trust God. Some people would call this foolishness, but that's what faith is: believing what God says despite the circumstances.

Second, Ruth finds the idea of returning to the false gods of Moab absolutely unthinkable. Now knowing the true God, she sees the emptiness of life apart from Him. Did that happen to you when you placed your genuine faith in God? I hope so because that insight is a sign of true faith.

God calls us to a life of faith, hope, and trust. He expects us to believe in His existence and obey His commandments even when others persecute and ridicule us. It's not always popular to believe in God or be loyal to Jesus. Just look at the lives of the prophets or the disciples!

LEARNING ALERT

Just as a shepherd protects his sheep, the Lord is your Shepherd who protects you. He will not desert you when your enemies surround you. He will be at your side on your saddest of days. He is encouraging us on in anticipation of our spending eternity with Him!

Lord, let us learn from Ruth. Fortify our faith through whatever trials we face today and in the future. You will never turn against us even when we feel like Naomi when she said, "The hand of the LORD has gone against me." You are always for us! Let us believe in You and be strengthened and encouraged. May we never return to our old gods. Amen!

Discussion Questions

1. When in your life, if ever, was there a time when nothing was going right? Share a few details.

2. What helped you deal with the sense of hopelessness? What did you do? How, if at all, did people help?

3. Think of a time when someone stuck close to you when you were dealing with difficulties. What did that person say or do? What was most helpful?

LESSON 19
Dealing with Pain

Ruth 1:19-22

> *So they both went until they came to Bethlehem. And when they had come to Bethlehem, all the city was stirred because of them, and the women said, "Is this Naomi?" She said to them, "Do not call me Naomi; call me Mara, for the Almighty has dealt very bitterly with me. I went out full, but the LORD has brought me back empty. Why do you call me Naomi, since the LORD has witnessed against me and the Almighty has afflicted me?"*

> *So Naomi returned, and with her Ruth the Moabitess, her daughter-in-law, who returned from the land of Moab. And they came to Bethlehem at the beginning of barley harvest.*
> *Ruth 1:19-22*

Nothing will keep Ruth from staying with her mother-in-law and journeying to Bethlehem. Ruth does not want to return to her old life and her former gods. The true God of Israel has saved her.

And Ruth is saved the same way we are in the New Testament era. She isn't saved because she obeyed the Law of Moses and participated in Jewish rituals. Works don't earn anyone salvation.

As Ruth hears the message of God about the coming Messiah, God helps her recognize the truth. So, by faith,

Ruth receives the grace of God. And her heart is changed from the inside out. She takes Naomi's God as her God, and her heart is turned toward Him. The beauty of how God saves individuals and changes them from the inside out never ceases to amaze me.

CASE IN POINT

I recently heard the testimony of a woman named Gwen who became a Christian as a young adult. She had been searching for spiritual truth, and prompting someone to search, is definitely the work of God in an unbeliever's heart.

A Christian friend shared the gospel with Gwen, who was intrigued but not ready to make a commitment. Through various subsequent circumstances, Gwen found herself ready to surrender to Christ. In the privacy of her bedroom, she bowed her head and prayed to God.

When she raised her head from prayer, Gwen said, she instantly saw the world through a different lens. When she went outside the house, everything was different. Her philosophy of life, her point of view on issues, and her feelings toward people were now different. She experienced the power of a loving God who changes us from the inside out.

God used a faithful friend in Gwen's life, a friend who, acting in love, was led by the Spirit to share the gospel with Gwen. And I believe this is what happened to Ruth. God used Naomi's influence and words along with God's power to draw Ruth toward Himself. The result is Ruth's heart of surrender, clear evidence of God's power to save.

The Bible says, *Abraham believed, God and it was reckoned to him as righteousness* (Galatians 3:6). As He did with Abraham, God deems Ruth righteous. Now she views the world differently, and faithfulness to her God is now the focus of her life.

"DO NOT CALL ME NAOMI"

So, together, Naomi and Ruth return to Naomi's home, Bethlehem. *And when they had come to Bethlehem, all the city stirred because of it, and the women said, "Is this Naomi?"* (verse 19).

In this small, agrarian village, Naomi's return after a 10-year absence causes some excitement. When she hears her name, Naomi tells the people, *"Do not call me Naomi; call me Mara, [meaning "bitter"], for the Almighty has dealt very bitterly with me."* No doubt, Naomi shares the entire painful story.

I believe Naomi is a God-fearing woman, but she is experiencing a crisis in her faith. I'm sure she believes in God's sovereignty and wonders why He has allowed this loss. She sees her adversity and pain as evidence of God's displeasure with her. As a result, bitterness makes its way into Naomi's heart.

I COME BACK EMPTY

Naomi describes her current state to the people of Bethlehem like this:

> *I went out full [with a husband and two sons], but the LORD has brought me back empty. Why do you call me Naomi since the LORD has witnessed against me and the Almighty has afflicted me?*
> Ruth 1:21

Naomi sees God as One who abandoned her and worked against her. Naomi's outlook is bleak, her faith is weak, and her hope is all but gone. She is walking by *sight,* not by *faith.* And we've all been there.

KEEP PEDALING

I know of a man who has faced many tragedies. His daughter died unexpectedly, his brother died after a long, painful illness, and two other family obligations required him to reconfigure his daily life for years.

When asked how his Christian faith has held up, he responded with a story. "I love to ride my bicycle. Sometimes I take long trips, and part of the course will seem like it's straight uphill. As I'm slowly making it up the incline, I pass by fellow cyclists who quit. They're younger than I am. They're in better shape. They're more experienced.

"So I'm sometimes asked how I'm able to make it to the top of the mountain. I guess it's because I know that all I can do—all I have to do—is pedal one more time. Then pedal another time. And then another. And I know that if I don't stop pedaling one more time, sooner or later, I'll make it to the top.

"I don't understand many things about what's happened in my life or why God allowed it to happen. But I'm going to trust Him. All I know to do is to keep pedaling. I don't have to understand everything right now. I just have to trust and pedal."

When we Christians suffer, we often come to a crossroads in our faith. Will we view God with bitterness, or will we accept suffering by faith, knowing that God is at work in our lives to do "good" things? After all, Romans 8:28 teaches that the Lord *causes all things to work together for good*. And we don't define the good; God does.

So trials come and with them loss and pain. But God will never give us more than we can—relying on His strength—endure, and He will always use that suffering and difficulty to strengthen us. That *is* good!

Those words may sound trite if you're going through a dark time right now. I know it's difficult to live with hope in moments of pain.

I pray you also know those times when God sees it best to bless us with healing, with happiness, with protection, and with the good things in this world. The good things of this world are temporary, yet they are good. At His discretion, God blesses us with the good things of this world when He deems it best. That also is good.

So let's surrender to our loving God and His definition of *good*.

LEARNING ALERT

Little does Naomi realize that God is using these difficult circumstances to set the stage for blessings upon blessings upon blessings. Some days seem like Crucifixion Friday when the disciples felt as if their hopes were dashed forever. But have faith! Resurrection Sunday is coming!

Lord, keep us from becoming bitter toward You. When we suffer, grant us an extra measure of faith. Let us lift our eyes and see You in all Your glory, power, and love. Let us not be like Job's wife who said, "Curse God and die" (Job 2:9). Instead, let us believe as Job did: "Shall we indeed accept good from God and not accept adversity?" In all this Job did not sin with his lips" (verse 10). Lift our hearts and our minds up to the heavens with a view toward Your plan of eternal blessings. Amen!

Discussion Questions

1. What are your thoughts about why God allows bad things to happen to Christians?

2. As Christians, what is bad and what is good when it comes to real-life situations? Be specific.

3. Describe a painful or difficult situation—ideally in your life or in the life of someone you know—that turned out to be a blessing far greater than you would have imagined.

LARRY SHAFFER

LESSON 20
Ruth's Faith in Action

Ruth 2:1-4

> *Now Naomi had a kinsman of her husband, a man of*
> *great wealth, of the family of Elimelech, whose name was*
> *Boaz. And Ruth the Moabitess said to Naomi, "Please*
> *let me go to the field and glean among the ears of grain*
> *after one in whose sight I may find favor."*
>
> *And she said to her, "Go, my daughter." So she departed*
> *and went and gleaned in the field after the reapers;*
> *and she happened to come to the portion of the field*
> *belonging to Boaz, who was of the family of Elimelech*
> *Now behold, Boaz came from Bethlehem and said to the*
> *reapers, "May the LORD be with you." And they said to*
> *him, "May the LORD bless you."*
> Ruth 2:1-4

The stage is set....

Naomi returns home to Bethlehem feeling abandoned by
God. Ruth, her daughter-in-law, returns with her. Although
a foreigner, Ruth has felt drawn to the God of Israel, so much
so that she no longer feels at home in her own country. She
has embraced Naomi's God as her God and Naomi's people
as her people.

The two widows settle in Bethlehem, but this time
Naomi doesn't live in the nice part of town. She is without

a man to provide for her, and she is too old to marry. Ruth is in a foreign land without a viable dating website to help her find the needle in a haystack of a man who will marry a foreigner. They are living on very humble means. But, as the Bible reports, *they came to Bethlehem at the beginning of barley harvest* (Ruth 1:22). And—providentially—this is a good time to return to Israel. I'll explain later.

IT'S OFF TO WORK WE GO

Ruth is probably in her early to mid-twenties); she is definitely healthy and industrious. She wants to do all she can to provide for Naomi and herself. So she says to Naomi, *"Please let me go to the field and glean among the ears of grain after one in whose sight I may find favor"* (Ruth 2:2). *Gleaning* was the act of picking up the stalks of grain left behind by the workers after the first cutting of the harvest.

Mosaic Law commands harvesters to not harvest the far corners of their land and to not pick up the gleanings that fall to the ground (Leviticus 23:22). These were to be left for the orphans, the widows, and the poor. Being a foreigner puts Ruth at a distinct disadvantage, but she hopes and prays that one of the farmers will look upon her with favor and welcome her to his field. By faith, she sets out to provide for Naomi and herself.

I know a little about the kind of situation Ruth finds herself in. When I was in my early thirties, I felt led to leave youth ministry and begin a career in business. I had a wife, two daughters, and a mortgage. I was fully responsible to provide for my family—and I had no business experience or education. Nevertheless, I found a sales job that paid primarily in commission. I rose early every morning, worked hard all day, faced rejection after rejection, came home at night, and spent time with my family. After everyone went to bed, I often spent time on my knees. Then, the next morning, I rose early and did the same thing all over again.

I experienced hopelessness, regrets over my decisions, and a heavy uncertainty about the future. It was a dark, difficult time. But—I saw later—it was a time that forged my character and galvanized positive qualities such as my faith, perseverance, and grit. Similarly, this season was a difficult time in my marriage, but Leigh and I see that the struggle strengthened our relationship. But, bottom line, when the odds are stacked against you as they were against Ruth, simply move forward one step at a time and do what needs to be done in the moment. Faith in God and the choice to persevere can make you invincible!

Ruth and Naomi are in a bad spot, but Ruth takes the initiative to make things better: Ruth acts. She doesn't sit around complaining. She actively tries to improve her situation. She is an amazing example of faith in God and perseverance. There is much we can learn from Ruth!

LEARNING ALERT

When have you been in a bad spot with no solution in sight? That is Ruth's situation, and she takes action, giving you and me a good example to follow. May we—as Ruth does—trust in God, not give up, persevere, remain faithful, and remember that He is with us and He will provide.

Lord, help us learn from Ruth! She seems to live with a strong sense of Your presence and confidence that You will lead her, use her, bless her, and keep her. But she doesn't just sit back and wait for You to give. With humility and respect, she acts. May we also exhibit our faith in You with our action: may we follow You, listen to You, and, with humility, depend on You while we move forward. May we remember that what we see with our physical eyes is not all that there is. We don't see it, but You are always at work and acting on our behalf. May we live by faith in You and not by sight. Amen!

Discussion Questions

1. What connection do you see between God's providence and our attitudes and actions?

2. James 1:12 connects our love for God to perseverance in trials. How does our love for God fuel perseverance?

3. Describe an example of extreme perseverance that you've seen in your life. What fueled that person's perseverance?

LESSON 21
The Kindness of Boaz

Ruth 2:5-13

Then Boaz said to his servant who was in charge of the reapers, "Whose young woman is this?" The servant in charge of the reapers replied, "She is the young Moabite woman who returned with Naomi from the land of Moab. And she said, 'Please let me glean and gather after the reapers among the sheaves.' Thus she came and has remained from the morning until now; she has been sitting in the house for a little while."

Then Boaz said to Ruth, "Listen carefully, my daughter. Do not go to glean in another field; furthermore, do not go on from this one, but stay here with my maids. Let your eyes be on the field which they reap and go after them. Indeed, I have commanded the servants not to touch you. When you are thirsty, go to the water jars and drink from what the servants draw." Then she fell on her face, bowing to the ground and said to him, "Why have I found favor in your sight that you should take notice of me, since I am a foreigner?" Boaz replied to her, "All that you have done for your mother-in-law after the death of your husband has been fully reported to me, and how you left your father and your mother and the land of your birth, and came to a people that you did not previously know. May the LORD reward your work, and your wages be full from the LORD, the God of Israel, under whose wings you have come to seek refuge." Then she said, "I have found favor in your sight,

> *my lord, for you have comforted me and indeed have*
> *spoken kindly to your maidservant, though I am not like*
> *one of your maidservants."*
> *Ruth 2:5-13*

Ruth finds the fields owned by Boaz, a kinsman of her deceased father-in-law. Yes, Ruth is a foreigner—a pagan Moabitess—and a widow. She is also known in Bethlehem as kind, humble, unselfish, and loyal. In the fields, the servants see that she is an industrious hard worker. Her newfound faith in the true God of Israel gives her confidence that He will care for her and her mother-in-law, Naomi. By faith—and rather than just sitting around—Ruth takes action and trusts that God will bless them in His time and His way.

THE BOSS IS HERE!

Toward the end of this particular workday, after Ruth has worked hard gleaning, Boaz arrives at the field he owns. As Boaz greets his workers with kind words of blessings, he notices Ruth in the distance. He asks his servant, *"Whose young woman is this?"* The servant in charge of the reapers replies, *"She is the young Moabite woman who returned with Naomi from the land of Moab"* (Ruth 2:5-6). After asking for permission to glean, the servant explains and he says, *"Thus, she came and has remained from the morning until now"* (verse 7).

A GOOD REPUTATION GOES A LONG WAY

Feeling compassion for Ruth, Boaz approaches her and tells her to stay in his field and glean. He assures her he will let all his servants know that she is welcome. He also tells Ruth that if she needs water, she may drink from the water jars and eat the food he has made available to his servants. Ruth falls on her face with gratitude and says, *"Why have I found favor in your sight that you should take notice of me, since I am a foreigner?"* (verse 10).

Here is Boaz's reply:

All that you have done for your mother-in-law after the death of your husband has been fully reported to me, and how you left your father and your mother and the land of your birth and came to a people that you did not previously know. May the LORD *reward your work, and your wages be full from the* LORD, *the God of Israel, under whose wings you have come to seek refuge.* (verses 11-12)

AN EXQUISITE PAINTING

Wow! What an exquisite painting of God's plan of redemption for His faithful servants.

First are the brilliant colors of God's sovereign and gracious provision for a humble, faithful widow who isn't even one of His chosen people.

Second, the picture is enhanced by the radiant shades of Ruth's sincere faith in the God of Israel. Her kind service to her mother-in-law and her diligent work add brilliance to this masterpiece.

Finally, we see the bright colors of Boaz's tender compassion to his workers and servants, compassion that he extends to a widowed Moabitess. In Boaz we see—and will come to see more clearly—God's heart of redeeming love. God has blessed Boaz, but his wealth has not turned him inward or made him arrogant or self-reliant. His faith in God is strong, his character is solid, and his kindness extends to all. Boaz foreshadows the work of the Messiah who will extend spiritual grace and redemption to all!

THE GOOD SAMARITAN'S DECISION

The kindness and character of Boaz reminds me of a story Jesus Himself told, a story that offers another portrait of God's grace and kindness.

A man from Samaria was walking along a very dangerous stretch of the 18-mile road between Jerusalem and Jericho. He came across another Jewish man who had been beaten and robbed. To say that the Samaritans and Jews did not like each other is an understatement. So, the Samaritan had a decision to make. Should he help this guy?

Jesus has said that two previous passers-by had decided not to help. Ironically, one was a priest and the other, a temple official. But the Samaritan stopped, an act that was risky; an act that cost him time and money. And this Samaritan is the example Jesus gives us as He calls us to love our neighbors. A neighbor is anyone we see in need, and we are good neighbors when we show compassion and take action to help.

So, I have a few questions about the Samaritan.

Why was the very fact he stopped to help unusual?

What was the risk?

Was this a convenient stop?

Was this an easy assignment?

Did he have the money to spare?

How does this apply to you and me?

And how does this parable of Jesus connect to the story of Boaz? Both exhibited kindness. Don't underestimate the power of kindness. True kindness is an outcome of the Spirit-filled life, (Galatians 5:22). Kindness is an attribute of God (Romans 2:4) and when we show true, unconditional kindness, we are displaying the beautiful character of our God. You and I have those same opportunities to show the image of God through kindness.

LEARNING ALERT

God paints an exquisite portrait of redemption not only in Ruth's life, but in our lives as well. He blends beautiful colors into a perfect picture—and how should we respond to God's redemption? Our responsibilities are simple: *What does the LORD require of you but to do justice, to love kindness, and to walk humbly with your God?* (Micah 6:8).

Lord, we want to have the compassion and generous heart of Boaz. We ask You to help us to act justly, to love kindness, and to walk humbly *with You. We are grateful that You are just as ready to use us—the way You used Boaz—to shine Your light and share Your love. Amen!*

Discussion Questions

1. Describe a time or two when you felt as if God had forgotten you. What finally showed you that He hadn't?

2. If we're honest, we all have times when we feel we have enough problems of our own without trying to help someone else. What do you think God would say to us in that situation?

3. Look back over your life. List specific times God used these colors in that painting—and praise Him!

    *   His sovereignty

    *   Grace

    *   Faith

    *   Kindness

    *   Compassion

    *   Love

LARRY SHAFFER

LESSON 22
A Love Story

Ruth 2

> *At mealtime Boaz said to her, "Come here, that you may eat of the bread and dip your piece of bread in the vinegar." So she sat beside the reapers; and he served her roasted grain, and she ate and was satisfied and had some left. When she rose to glean, Boaz commanded his servants, saying, "Let her glean even among the sheaves, and do not insult her. Also you shall purposely pull out for her some grain from the bundles and leave it that she may glean, and do not rebuke her."*

> *So she gleaned in the field until evening. Then she beat out what she had gleaned, and it was about an ephah of barley. She took it up and went into the city, and her mother-in-law saw what she had gleaned. She also took it out and gave Naomi what she had left after she was satisfied. Her mother-in-law then said to her, "Where did you glean today and where did you work? May he who took notice of you be blessed." So she told her mother-in-law with whom she had worked and said, "The name of the man with whom I worked today is Boaz." Naomi said to her daughter-in-law, "May he be blessed of the LORD who has not withdrawn his kindness to the living and to the dead." Again Naomi said to her, "The man is our relative, he is one of our closest relatives." Then Ruth the Moabitess said, "Furthermore, he said to me, 'You should stay close to my servants until*

they have finished all my harvest.'" Naomi said to Ruth her daughter-in-law, "It is good, my daughter, that you go out with his maids, so that others do not fall upon you in another field." So she stayed close by the maids of Boaz in order to glean until the end of the barley harvest and the wheat harvest. And she lived with her mother-in-law.
Ruth 2:14-23

A love story is about to emerge. Oh, it's quite different from the movies that Hollywood produces. The foundation of this love story is a common faith in the true God of Israel. A man and a woman from two very different worlds share a common bond of humility, kindness, and a sincere faith in God.

SHE FOLLOWED HER HEART OF FAITH IN GOD

Ruth has moved to Bethlehem and assumed the responsibility of caring and providing for her widowed mother-in-law, Naomi. After the death of her own husband, Ruth could have returned to Moab and found security in remarrying. Instead Ruth chooses to do a very honorable thing. Following her heart—which is now filled with love for and faith in God—Ruth honors God by serving Naomi.

We hear the term *follow your heart* in everything from office gossip to reality TV shows. The message is basically, "Be true to what *you* want to do." In contrast, Ruth does what *God* wants her to do. That different orientation makes *all* the difference in the world.

HARVESTTIME

Harvesttime in Bethlehem provides a window of time for the widow, the orphan, and the poor to store up grain for the long winter. So Ruth goes to work, from morning to night, and gleans in the barley fields. As we've seen, Mosaic law requires farmers to leave the corners of the field unharvested and to not pick up stalks that fall to the side (Leviticus 23:22). This barley is to be left for the needy. As widows, Ruth and Naomi fit the bill.

YOU'VE BEEN PROMOTED!

When Naomi begins to glean in Boaz's field, he notices her and realizes she is kin through marriage. Boaz is a very close relative of Elimelech, Naomi's deceased husband and Ruth's father-in-law. As such, he extends extreme kindness to Ruth and welcomes her as one of his workers rather than just a widowed gleaner.

> At mealtime Boaz said to her, "Come here, that you may eat of the bread and dip your piece of bread in the vinegar." She sat beside the reapers, and he served her roasted grain, and she ate and was satisfied and had some left. When she rose to glean, Boaz commanded his servants, saying, "Let her glean even among the sheaves, and do not insult her. Also, you shall purposely pull out

for her some grain from the bundles and leave it that she may glean, and do not rebuke her."

"BLESSED ARE THE MEEK"

In Matthew 5:5, Jesus said, "Blessed are the meek, for they shall inherit the earth." That statement might not mean much to you and me. In fact, *meek* sounds a lot like mousy or weak. But the people Jesus was speaking to understood the word. *Meek*, for instance, described a soldier's horse that was trained to lead troops into battle, trample opposing forces, and clear the way for those soldiers who followed.

Yet this same horse would allow the soldier's young children to pull on its mane and tail. They could even walk under it without being harmed. Of course that horse could have easily hurt or killed the children, but it didn't. It was only aggressive on the battlefield when its master gave the command.

The horse was meek. And meekness is controlled strength. Meekness is power under control.

What does it mean for God's people to be meek? Like the horse, our strength is to be controlled. Being meek, then, is using our energy for good. For God. It's making the conscious choice to follow God's commands and live under His direction.

Even though he lived hundreds of years before Jesus spoke these words, Boaz personifies meekness. He chooses to use his power for good, for God. A humble servant of the Almighty, Boaz treats his servants well and shows concern and extends compassion to the widows.

Whether you realize it or not, you have that same opportunity. You have the opportunity to use all that is within you and at your disposal for good, for God!

THINGS ARE NOT ALWAYS AS THEY SEEM

Boaz is especially good to Ruth because he has heard about her kindness to Naomi as well as her newfound faith in the God of Israel. (Ruth 1:16)

So Ruth arrives home with a large portion of grain. Then she sits with Naomi and shares the entire story—and Naomi is thrilled. She knows that having rich relatives can be a real plus when you find yourself in poverty.

Not long ago, Naomi had felt that God's curse was upon her. It *felt* that way to Naomi, but God hadn't cursed her. God is always in charge and fulfilling His good plan for His children's lives. Admittedly, His plan is different from what Naomi envisioned before her husband and her sons died. Nevertheless, it was God's plan to use Naomi and Ruth as a blessing to many in the future, and Boaz's kindness to Ruth on her first day of gleaning is a spark of newfound hope for Naomi and Ruth. The next morning, filled with hope, Naomi shares a master plan with Ruth. God is at work, and His providential plan is amazing.

More next time.

LEARNING ALERT

God wants the same response from you and me that we see in Boaz. God wants us to love our neighbors as ourselves. He expects us to serve others with compassion, generosity, and humility. And, just as Boaz does, we should seek opportunities to help others.

Lord, please give us the faith we need to trust in You even when we can't clearly see or begin to understand Your plan. We want to trust You regardless of our circumstances. Amen!

Discussion Questions

1. Why can the encouragement to follow your heart be dangerous or at least less than helpful advice for a Christian?

2. Now that we understand what Jesus means by meek, whom do you know or know of who is an example of meekness, who lives with power under control? What enables that person and what motivates that person to keep power under control?

3. What is the substance of or foundation for Naomi's newfound hope?

LESSON 23
The Plan

Ruth 3:1-9

Then Naomi, her mother-in-law, said to her, "My daughter, shall I not seek security for you, that it may be well with you? Now is not Boaz our kinsman, with whose maids you were? Behold, he winnows barley at the threshing floor tonight. Wash yourself therefore, and anoint yourself and put on your best clothes, and go down to the threshing floor; but do not make yourself known to the man until he has finished eating and drinking. It shall be when he lies down, that you shall notice the place where he lies, and you shall go and uncover his feet and lie down; then he will tell you what you shall do." She said to her, "All that you say I will do."

So she went down to the threshing floor and did according to all that her mother-in-law had commanded her. When Boaz had eaten and drunk and his heart was merry, he went to lie down at the end of the heap of grain; and she came secretly and uncovered his feet and lay down. It happened in the middle of the night that the man was startled and bent forward; and behold, a woman was lying at his feet. He said, "Who are you?" And she answered, "I am Ruth your maid. So spread your covering over your maid, for you are a close relative."
Ruth 3:1-9

When have life's trials and difficulties made you wonder if a black cloud would hang over you forever? Such has been Naomi's situation. Consequently, Ruth becomes companion and provider. Ruth puts the needs of her mother-in-law before her own.

Ruth has found favor with Boaz. She is working hard to glean enough grain to sustain Naomi and herself in the coming year. The black cloud doesn't seem quite so ominous.

AN ODD CUSTOM

The next morning Naomi shares a plan with Ruth, a plan that will change Ruth's status from that of a widowed foreigner. The plan involves a Near Eastern custom that seems very odd to us in the 21st-century West. The plan will require courage and initiative on Ruth's part. Let me explain.

As a close kinsman to Ruth through marriage, Boaz has the option—and it's not a requirement—to marry Ruth and redeem her from the difficult life of a widow in the unfamiliar land of Israel. But because Boaz is older than Ruth, it would not be honorable for him to propose. So Naomi sets forth the plan:

> *Now is not Boaz our kinsman?... Behold, he winnows barley at the threshing floor tonight. Wash yourself therefore, and anoint yourself and put on your best clothes, and go down to the threshing floor... It shall be when he lies down, that you should notice the place*

where he lies, and you shall go and uncover his feet and lie down; then he will tell you what to do."
Ruth 3:2-4

If this plan seems very forward, do your best to look at this plan in the context of the culture. Also consider that two very honorable, God-fearing people are involved. This plan that Naomi describes will allow Ruth to show her desire to be redeemed by Boaz without drawing attention or risking the shame of being denied.

WILL YOU MARRY ME?

Ruth goes to the threshing floor and waits until after Boaz has eaten. When he lies down, she quietly uncovers his feet and lays down near them. Later in the night Boaz awakens and is startled that a woman is at his feet.

[Boaz] said, "Who are you?" And she answered, "I am Ruth your maid. So, spread your covering over your maid, for you are a close relative."

Boaz knows that Ruth is proposing that he marry her and become her kinsman-redeemer. And we'll come back to this.

The Power of Initiative

I'm drawn to the initiative of Naomi and Ruth. I can't help but reflect on my years of famine and dark clouds—and then God broke through.

I wrote that, despite hard work and diligence, my first couple of years in the business world after ministry were very lean financially and very, very difficult. But, after those two years of business failures, God opened the floodgates and poured blessing after blessing into my professional life. My former college roommate called me out of the blue and offered me a job. I would have significant responsibilities— and a solid salary that was about three times what I had made during my years as a salesman. I asked him why he was willing to offer me such an important job when I had absolutely no experience. First, he said, he was sure I would learn the business. Second, he explained, what he really needed was someone he could trust, someone with integrity and character. How could I have known that the way I lived in college would turn out to be the most important job interview of my life?

No longer wondering when I'd next close a sale or be able to pay a bill, I chose this time in my life to set long-range goals and plans for my life. I remember the tension I felt between setting lofty and very specific goals *and* knowing in my heart that I should always be willing to surrender to God. I very much wanted to be successful, but I wanted success to come God's way, not mine. So, prayerfully, I took the initiative and set a long-term plan for my life—and I call that "prayerful initiative."

During that period of my life, I wrote and outlined plans for my family life, my professional life, and my life of service. From that work emerged detailed goals and governing values for my life. Additionally, I defined my Life Mission, and it has remained unchanged for over 25 years.

My Life Mission: To be a man of God.

I am passionate about my purpose in life, which is to enjoy an intimate, personal relationship with God through the Lord Jesus Christ and by the power of the Holy Spirit.

- Enjoy and be a blessing to my family

- Be used by God to reach, touch, and positively affect people's lives for eternity

- Build and grow strong businesses that provide valuable services

- Be financially secure and independent

- Extensively fund missionary endeavors around the world

- Travel and pursue ministry opportunities

- Live a life of adventure

I would guess that, as she gleans, Ruth is hoping and praying for a new life free of the difficulties of widowhood and the poverty that comes with it. I believe it's honorable to live that way—to always look for opportunities to improve my life, to improve the life of those I love, and to give to those in need. With an eye toward heaven and an ear tuned to God's leading, may we take the initiative to serve Him in our family, at our workplace, and in our community and the world.

LEARNING ALERT

A God-honoring life of purpose requires us to be prayerful, to examine our motives, and to walk humbly as our heavenly Father guides. We're seeing an example of this unfold. Neither Naomi's plan nor Ruth's follow-through is initiated for selfish purposes. Instead, both are carried out according to the Lord's promptings and His plan.

Lord, You open doors; You present opportunities; You lead. May we—like Naomi and Ruth—be prayerful and attentive to Your guidance so that we will engage in noble pursuits with initiative and courage. Amen!

Discussion Questions

1. When black clouds appear overhead, what would you like your response to be? What can you do when the sun is shining to prepare yourself to respond like that?

2. Would you describe yourself as being a person of initiative? Why or why not? And why do you think you're like that?

3. What is your definition of "prayerful initiative"? When have you taken prayerful initiative in your life? Are you glad you did? Why or why not? Do you have an opportunity right now to prayerfully take initiative in some aspect of your life?

LESSON 24
A Special Young Woman

Ruth 3:9-11

> *[Boaz] said, "Who are you?" And she answered, "I am Ruth your maid. So spread your covering over your maid, for you are a close relative."*
>
> *Then he said, "May you be blessed of the LORD, my daughter. You have shown your last kindness to be better than the first by not going after young men, whether poor or rich. Now, my daughter, do not fear. I will do for you whatever you ask, for all my people in the city know that you are a woman of excellence."*
> Ruth 3:9-11

Remember when Boaz first meets Ruth while she is gleaning in his field? He blesses her and says, *"May the LORD reward your work, and your wages be full from the LORD, the God of Israel, under whose wings you have come to seek refuge"* (Ruth 2:12).

Little does Boaz know that God will use him to fulfill the very prayer he has prayed for Ruth.

According to Naomi's plan, Ruth discreetly goes to Boaz at night, uncovers his feet, and asks him to spread his cover over her since he is a close relative. This correlates to Boaz' blessing that Ruth has put her faith in God, *"under whose wings she has come to seek refuge."* As mentioned, this Near Eastern custom indicates Ruth's desire for her close relative—but not a blood relative—to marry her and, because she is a widow in a foreign land, to redeem her from the challenges of widowhood.

HOW DOES BOAZ RESPOND?

Awakened in the middle of the night, Boaz hears a life-changing proposal—and God must have been preparing his heart. Without hesitating, Boaz immediately responds:

> *May you be blessed of the LORD, my daughter. You have shown your last kindness to be better than the first by not going after young men, whether poor or rich. Now, my daughter, do not fear. I will do for you whatever you ask, for all my people in the city know that you are a woman of excellence."*

GREAT-GRANDSON SOLOMON

Boaz acknowledges that Ruth is a *woman of excellence*, and all the people of the village agree. We can agree with Boaz's description as well. This remarkable young woman is indeed a woman of excellence. What, however, are some specific and timeless characteristics of such a woman?

The best answer to that question that I know of was offered approximately 120 years after Boaz utters these words. That is when—spoiler alert—Ruth's great-grandson Solomon penned Proverbs 31. This detailed description of a woman of excellence begins this way:

> *An excellent wife, who can find?*
> *For her worth is far above jewels.*
> *The heart of her husband trusts her,*
> *And he will have no lack of gain.*

We'll look at Proverbs 31 in greater detail next time.

LEARNING ALERT

A few years ago I asked myself, *How can I strengthen my walk with the Lord and, in terms of my character, become more like Jesus?*

1. Church and fellowship. In the original language, it's called the assembly of the righteous. One of the reasons it was established was so we could encourage and strengthen each other. Through worship, Bible studies, small groups and fellowship, this has proven true for me.

2. Personal Study and Devotions. When I became intentional in my study of God's Word, my faith and relationship with Him grew. By that, I created a time each day to read and pray. I determined what I would devote myself to in God's Word and daily prayer. Even if it's a short time, I did it daily.

3. An Accountability Partner. As I have previously mentioned, my accountability partner has provided challenge and encouragement. It's a real blessing and one I would encourage for you to think about.

Lord, may You strengthen our resolve as we seek to live a life that honors You. May You guide our lives. Amen

Discussion Questions

1. Do you have a committed Bible study/prayer time each day? If not, consider why that's the case. If so, evaluate what you're doing and why. Either way, ask God to give you a passion for this time and guidance as to what He would have you study.

2. Who in your life is a person of excellence? Why does he/she earn those words of honor? Be specific.

3. What areas of spiritual discipline would you like to improve?

LESSON 25
A Woman of Excellence

Ruth 3 and Proverbs 31

PRAISE FOR A GOOD WOMAN

An excellent wife, who can find?
For her worth is far above jewels.
The heart of her husband trusts in her,
And he will have no lack of gain.
She does him good and not evil
All the days of her life.
She looks for wool and flax
And works with her hands in delight.
She is like merchant ships;
She brings her food from afar.
She rises also while it is still night
And gives food to her household
And portions to her maidens.
She considers a field and buys it;
From her earnings she plants a vineyard.
She girds herself with strength
And makes her arms strong.
She senses that her gain is good;
Her lamp does not go out at night.
She stretches out her hands to the distaff,
And her hands grasp the spindle.
She extends her hand to the poor,
And she stretches out her hands to the needy.

She is not afraid of the snow for her household,
For all her household are clothed with scarlet.
She makes coverings for herself;
Her clothing is fine linen and purple.
Her husband is known in the gates,
When he sits among the elders of the land.
She makes linen garments and sells them,
And supplies belts to the tradesmen.
Strength and dignity are her clothing,
And she smiles at the future.
She opens her mouth in wisdom,
And the teaching of kindness is on her tongue.
She looks well to the ways of her household,
And does not eat the bread of idleness.
Her children rise up and bless her;
Her husband also, and he praises her, saying:
"Many daughters have done nobly,
But you excel them all."
Charm is deceitful and beauty is vain,
But a woman who fears the Lord, she shall
be praised.
Give her the product of her hands,
And let her works praise her in the gates.
Proverbs 31:10-31

Boaz describes Ruth as a woman of excellence. Approximately 120 years later, Ruth's great-grandson Solomon wrote Proverbs 31, a chapter that describes a woman of excellence. Perhaps the legacy of Ruth's fine qualities was a legacy passed down from generation to generation.

LOVE AND RESPECT

After declaring *her worth... far beyond jewels*, the writer comments on this excellent woman's role as a wife:

> *The heart of her husband trusts in her...*
> *She does him good and not evil*
> *All the days of her life.*
> Proverbs 31:11-12

Nothing changed between Solomon's writing of Proverbs 31 and Paul's writing of Ephesians 5. There the apostle stated that a husband should, above all else, love his wife—and to be deeply loved is a wife's deepest yearning. Paul had a word for wives as well: *The wife must see to it that she respects her husband* (Ephesians 5:33). Without a doubt, a husband's deepest need is his wife's respect.

Of course husbands and wives need both love and respect. But the primary focus for husbands is to love their wives. The primary focus for wives—for excellent wives—is to respect their husbands. When a man is respected by his wife, he will go out into the world with confidence that he can do anything! He will soar!

HER GAIN IS GOOD

Even with only a quick skim of Proverbs 31, readers know that a woman of excellence is industrious. She works hard and delights in serving her family, but she also is in the marketplace earning some income.

> *"She looks for wool and flax*
> *And works with her hands in delight....*
> *She rises also while it is still night*
> *And gives food to her household...*
> *She considers a field and buys it;*
> *From her earnings she plants a vineyard....*
> *She senses that her gain is good.*
> *Her lamp does not go out at night.*
> Proverbs 31:13, 15-16, 18

She endlessly takes initiative to better herself and her family. Her diligence and hard work seem to bring her much confidence and a sense of significance. Her substantial contributions to her husband and children fuel her joy and her willingness to do even more.

SHE IS KIND

Evidence of her industriousness is her effort to clothe her family and herself with fine linen.

> *All her household are clothed with scarlet.*
> *She makes coverings for herself;*
> *Her clothing is fine linen and purple.*
> Proverbs 31:21-22

This excellent woman's confidence and success do not lead to pride and snootiness. She remains imminently kind:

> *She extends her hand to the poor,*
> *And she stretches out her hands to the needy....*
> *She opens her mouth in wisdom,*

And the teaching of kindness is on her tongue."
Proverbs 31:20, 26

As much as she gets done in a day, this woman of excellence is never too busy to be kind.

SHE FEARS THE LORD

Foundational to this woman's excellence is her fear and reverence for God:

> *Charm is deceitful, and beauty is vain,*
> *But a woman who fears [reveres] the LORD, she*
> *shall be praised.*
> Proverbs 31:30

Boaz says to Ruth, *"All my people in the city know that you are a woman of excellence"* (Ruth 3:11). An excellent woman's reputation cannot be suppressed. Her life will prompt the respect of all who know her.

LEARNING ALERT

In light of this overview of an excellent woman, consider God's instruction to us in Colossians 3:23:

> *Whatever you do, do your work heartily,*
> *as for the Lord rather than for men.*

We honor God when we live with love, when we aim for excellence, and when we do to the best of our ability whatever He calls us to do.

Consider this story about a man who was hired to build a very fine house for a very rich man. The contractor had a set amount of time to finish the house. He was told that the client would be gone during construction, and he would receive no supervision as he worked. The builder was simply trusted to make the house the very best he could.

When the client returned, he met the contractor at the finished house. After the contractor showed the client around, he handed over the keys. To the contractor's great surprise, the client gave him back the keys.

"It's yours," he said. "I don't need it, and I want you to have it."

The contractor didn't know what to say. And for weeks, months, and even years afterward, he thought about his client's generosity. He also thought about a few corners he'd cut. If he were to build the house again, he definitely wouldn't have cut those corners... because he would have been building his own house.

You probably see the analogy. God wants us to treat others the way we want to be treated. He wants us to reflect His character by being honest, compassionate, generous, unselfish, and kind.

Lord, may we consider the example of Ruth and seek to live a life that both honors You and blesses those we meet. Amen!

Discussion Questions

1. Who in your life, if anyone, has been a Boaz and helped you in ways you could never repay? Describe what that person did—and why.

2. What might you do to prepare to be a Ruth or Boaz? Does it just come naturally? What skills could be learned and sharpened?

3. What qualities do you admire most in Ruth? In Boaz? Be specific on both counts.

LESSON 26
There's a Catch...

Ruth 3:12-18

> *"Now it is true I am a close relative; however, there is a relative closer than I. Remain this night, and when morning comes, if he will redeem you, good; let him redeem you. But if he does not wish to redeem you, then I will redeem you, as the LORD lives. Lie down until morning."*
>
> *So she lay at his feet until morning and rose before one could recognize another; and he said, "Let it not be known that the woman came to the threshing floor." Again he said, "Give me the cloak that is on you and hold it." So she held it, and he measured six measures of barley and laid it on her. Then she went into the city. When she came to her mother-in-law, she said, "How did it go, my daughter?" And she told her all that the man had done for her. She said, "These six measures of barley he gave to me, for he said, 'Do not go to your mother-in-law empty-handed. Then she said, "Wait, my daughter, until you know how the matter turns out; for the man will not rest until he has settled it today."*
> Ruth 3:12-18

Boaz is thrilled that Ruth has come forward and let him know that she wants to marry him and be redeemed. Even though Ruth is a Moabite, a race despised by Israel, Boaz knows that her faith in God is genuine: her life and character testify to a truly redeemed soul. As such, Boaz is honored to take on the role of Ruth's physical redeemer, and he will do so in honor of his God who is already her spiritual redeemer. But, yes, there is a catch....

THE CLOSE RELATIVE

Hear Boaz's words to Ruth

> *Now it is true I am a close relative; however, there is a relative closer than I... if he will redeem you, good; let him redeem you. But if he does not wish to redeem you, then I will redeem you, as the LORD lives.*
> Ruth 3:12-13

An honorable man, Boaz does not hesitate to tell Ruth of the man in the village who is a closer relative to Ruth's deceased father in law than Boaz is. Boaz know well that the book of Leviticus gives the nearest relative first rights to redeem, (Leviticus 25:25).

Before he can proceed, Boaz must first give the closer kinsman the opportunity to marry Ruth. Boaz is determined to do the right thing and leave the results to God. Not having the resolution she would have liked, Ruth leaves Boaz, goes home, and tells her mother-in-law everything that had happened.

SITTING AND WONDERING

I'm sure Ruth was anxious—and understandably so. Will she marry a close relative she has never even met, or will she marry the kind and gentle Boaz? To sit and wonder about these two scenarios would certainly raise questions, stir up fear, and cause worry. Ever been there?

In such times, our tendency is to act with the hope of influencing the outcome. But what kind of action? Your mind searches for options: *What can I do? Whom should I talk to?*

Boaz is a busy man. Does she wonder, *How soon will I be able to talk to that relative? How long will I have to wait and sit here in uncertainty?*

Naomi comforts Ruth by saying, *"Wait, my daughter, until you know how the matter turns out; for the man will not rest until he has settled it today"* (Ruth 3:18).

WAITING AND RESTING IN GOD

Wait. Wait. Wait. No one likes to wait! And none of us want to have our future decided by the actions of someone else? If I don't wait and act, will my action to facilitate the process improve the outcome, or spoil every chance of success? To wait or not to wait?

Earlier, we discussed taking initiative, but doing so patiently and prayerfully under the guiding hand of God. In Ruth's current situation, we see that she's able to wait on the Lord. Which is better? To act or to wait?

To act or to wait? Most of the arguments I have with my wife are over the question of to act or wait when we or a loved one faces a difficult decision or situation. She is action-oriented, and I'm a wait-and-watch person. This difference has made for some… uh… lively and sometimes emotional discussions. Act or wait? Which is the right thing to do?

What to do depends on the situation, but we can learn from Ruth: she takes action as far as she is able. Ruth steps back to allow God to do as He sees fit.

THE POWERFUL SILENT ACTION

Unfortunately, we sometimes leave prayer to the last rather than go to God first. Another aspect of waiting for the Lord is prayer. Sometimes, after doing all we can do, we throw up our arms and say, "There's nothing else I can do now except pray."

Prayer is actually a critical part of God's plan of action for us even though it may seem more like inaction than action. We can often relate to David's words in Psalm 69:2-3:

> *I have sunk in deep mire, and there is no foothold;*
> *I have come into deep waters, and a flood overflows me.*
> *I am weary with my crying; my throat is parched;*
> *My eyes fail while I wait for my God.*

A recurring pattern in David's psalms is to open with an expression of his despair and even depression. He openly writes of his displeasure with God. It feels to David as if

God has abandoned him. But the closing verses of the psalm reveal that David comes to his senses and remembers the promises of God. This psalm that begins with despair now ends with hope and confidence. Psalms 69:29-30, 32 says:

> *May Your salvation, O God, set me securely on high.*
> *I will praise the name of God with song*
> *And magnify Him with thanksgiving....*
> *You who seek God, let your heart revive.*

THE RIGHT THING

So while Ruth waits on the Lord, Boaz takes action. He goes to talk to another relative about his opportunity to marry Ruth. Boaz does the right thing. Obeying God often means putting ourselves out there, and the cost can be high.

Ask Abraham when he learns who the sacrifice was going to be.

Ask Shadrach, Meshach, and Abednego when they refuse to bow down to the king.

Ask Daniel when he refuses to alter his prayer schedule.

LEARNING ALERT

What can we learn from Ruth and Boaz? We can follow their examples and prayerfully take the initiative and then prayerfully wait on the Lord.

Lord, may we be patient to wait on You when You call us to wait. We will need you because sometimes our greatest test of faith is to do nothing. May we also remember that whatever the future holds, the events in our lives are not haphazard or uncertain. Nothing—I mean, nothing—happens outside of Your divine plan. May we rest in You who are faithful and good. Give us, we pray, the wisdom to know when to act and when to wait. Amen!

Discussion Questions

1. Are you more action-oriented or more "wait and see?" Why do you think that is? When has the way you're wired served you well? When has it been challenging?

2. Can you relate to the pattern of David's psalm described above? When in your sadness or depression have you had the presence of mind to pray and found that your sadness became praise?

3. Proverbs 3:6 says, 'In all your ways acknowledge Him... What does this mean and how can you be more diligent to follow this directive?

LESSON 27
The Right Thing

Ruth 4:1-12

Now Boaz went up to the gate and sat down there, and behold, the close relative of whom Boaz spoke was passing by, so he said, "Turn aside, friend, sit down here." And he turned aside and sat down. He took ten men of the elders of the city and said, "Sit down here." So they sat down. Then he said to the closest relative, "Naomi, who has come back from the land of Moab, has to sell the piece of land which belonged to our brother Elimelech. So I thought to inform you, saying, 'Buy it before those who are sitting here, and before the elders of my people. If you will redeem it, redeem it; but if not, *tell me that I may know; for there is no one but you to redeem it, and I am after you.'" And he said, "I will redeem it." Then Boaz said, "On the day you buy the field from the hand of Naomi, you must also acquire Ruth the Moabitess, the widow of the deceased, in order to raise up the name of the deceased on his inheritance." The closest relative said, "I cannot redeem it for myself, because I would jeopardize my own inheritance. Redeem it for yourself; you may have my right of redemption, for I cannot redeem it."*

Now this was the custom in former times in Israel concerning the redemption and the exchange of land to confirm any matter: a man removed his sandal and gave it to another; and this was the manner of attestation in

Israel. So the closest relative said to Boaz, "Buy it for yourself." And he removed his sandal. Then Boaz said to the elders and all the people, "You are witnesses today that I have bought from the hand of Naomi all that belonged to Elimelech and all that belonged to Chilion and Mahlon. Moreover, I have acquired Ruth the Moabitess, the widow of Mahlon, to be my wife in order to raise up the name of the deceased on his inheritance, so that the name of the deceased will not be cut off from his brothers or from the court of his birth place; you are witnesses today."

All the people who were in the court, and the elders, said, "We are witnesses. May the LORD make the woman who is coming into your home like Rachel and Leah, both of whom built the house of Israel; and may you achieve wealth in Ephrathah and become famous in Bethlehem. Moreover, may your house be like the house of Perez whom Tamar bore to Judah, through the offspring which the LORD will give you by this young woman."
Ruth 4: 1-12

After Boaz promises to redeem Ruth, he moves on it immediately. Boaz goes to the gate of the city, where most business transactions take place, and waits for his close relative to pass by. Once Boaz finds his relative, he asks ten elders of the city to verify the transaction. The stage is set for a legitimate and legal discussion of redemption.

Boaz tells his relative that their kinsman's wife, Naomi, possesses land that she inherited from their brother, and she needs to sell it to provide for herself. The law sets forth that the land should be redeemed by a close relative in order to keep it in the family. At first, this more distant relative is interested in the land, but then Boaz tells him there was more. The daughter-in-law of their deceased kinsman is now part of the family, and, with the sale of the land, she will be the purchaser's wife. Thus, the land would remain in the family as well as the offspring of the new wife, Ruth.

I LOVE YOU TO THE MOON AND BACK

In response, the man first in line for the land and therefore for Ruth says, *"I cannot redeem for myself, because I would jeopardize my own inheritance. Redeem for yourself; you may have my right of redemption, for I cannot redeem."* He is interested in the property, but not in another wife.

So Boaz turns to the elders, repeats the terms of the transaction, and confirms his right to purchase the land and marry Ruth. For Boaz, this legal transaction is at the same time an act of love. Ruth has truly gripped his heart from the first time they met. He must now be over the moon!

THE PROPHETIC BLESSING

Before Boaz leaves the gate to share the good news with Ruth, the elders respond:

> *We are witnesses. May the LORD make the woman who is coming into your home like Rachel and Leah, both of*

whom built the house of Israel; and may you achieve wealth in Ephrathah and become famous in Bethlehem.

The elders bless the future offspring of Boaz and Ruth. This act is especially amazing in that Ruth is a Moabitess, not a Jew by birth. But the elders bless Ruth as if she has all the rights of a Jew. In addition, this blessing links her to Rachel and Leah, two of Israel's most significant matriarchs.

REDEEMED!

What a beautiful story! Even in circumstances of sadness, despair, and poverty, Ruth remains faithful to Naomi and to God. Although she doesn't know how her life will turn out, she knows God, the One who holds her life in His hands, and everyone knows of her trust in God.

Well, the outcome could not have been better! God has provided a redeemer, someone who loves her and will care for her just as our Redeemer, Jesus, loves us and cares for us. Boaz is a foreshadowing of Jesus. Just as Boaz does for Ruth, Jesus fulfills our legal obligation and secures our forgiveness of sin. And just like Boaz, Jesus does so out of love.

LEARNING ALERT

When Jesus spoke His final words from the cross—"*It is finished!*" (John 19:30)—our sin debt was paid; the transaction was complete. Jesus endured the wrath that we deserved and fulfilled our debt to God. Just as Boaz fulfills the obligation of kinsman-redeemer before the elders, Jesus fulfills His obligation as our kinsman-redeemer before God and before the hosts of heaven and hell. "*It is finished!*" Legal requirements have been met, an act fueled by eternal and divine love, kindness, and grace. What a Savior!

Lord, the book of Ruth offers a beautiful picture of what You have done for us. We are orphans, foreigners, rebels against You. Nevertheless, You redeem us and adopt us as Your child with full rights and privileges. Just as Boaz is Ruth's earthly kinsman-redeemer, You, Lord, are our spiritual Kinsman-Redeemer, and You make with us an eternal covenant of blessing. You are our Rescuer and our Hero. We love You, and we will thank You always. Amen!

Discussion Questions

1. As you understand it, what is Jesus' legal obligation as our Savior?

2. Does this account of the Ruth and Boaz story teach that Christians' lives will always have a happy ending? Explain—and clarify the take-aways from this story.

3. We know Boaz richly blesses Ruth. What blessings do we receive from Jesus? Be specific.

4. Look again at the elders' blessing. In what ways did their words prove to be prophetic? Be specific—and if you aren't sure, there are a couple more lessons!

LESSON 28
From Empty to Full

Ruth 4: 13-15

> *So Boaz took Ruth, and she became his wife, and he went into her. And the LORD enabled her to conceive, and she gave birth to a son. Then the women said to Naomi, "Blessed is the LORD who has not left you without a redeemer today, and may his name become famous in Israel. May he also be to you a restorer of life and a sustainer of your old age; for your daughter-in-law, who loves you and is better to you than seven sons, has given birth to him."*
> *Ruth 4:13-15*

Boaz successfully negotiates the legal terms of his right to redeem Naomi's land and to marry Ruth. Boaz fulfills the role of a kinsman-redeemer, so now both women have someone to provide for them.

Remember Naomi's words when she returned to her homeland after her husband and two sons died?

> *The Almighty has dealt very bitterly with me. I went out full, but the LORD has brought me back empty.... The LORD has witnessed against me and the Almighty has afflicted me.*
> Ruth 1:20-21

At this point, Naomi has no hope and no joy: the future looks bleak.

But today the joy of redemption has flooded Naomi's heart. She who proclaims, *"Blessed is the LORD who has not left you without a redeemer today"* (Ruth 4:14).

THE CHAIN IS UNBROKEN

The Almighty has also provided redemption for Ruth. Remember the elders' blessing when they confirm Boaz's legal right to marry Ruth? They said, *"May your house be like the house of Perez whom Tamar bore to Judah, through the offspring which the LORD will give you by this young woman"* (Ruth 4:12).

Then we read in verse 13 that <u>Ruth *gave birth to a son*.</u>

And that event is hugely significant. Why? The elders knew that Boaz is from the line of Judah—from the line of Abraham, Isaac, and Jacob. They knew, then, that Boaz's firstborn son would be in the line of the Messiah. If Boaz doesn't have a son, the line will be broken.

But the Lord enables Ruth to conceive a son. Just as God used the foreigner Tamar, God uses a redeemed Moabite widow to keep His covenant promise. What a story!

YOU PREPARED THE WAY

Clearly, long before Jesus was born, God was at work preparing to send His people the Messiah as He had promised. Because of the sin of Adam and Eve, we needed God's help. Sin had created a debt that humans could not repay. Knowing that, God planned to send a Redeemer...a Savior; someone to pay our debt, to bridge the gap between sinful human beings and our holy God, and to remove the veil between God and us... Someone who could kick a hole in the wall of death... Someone who could build us a new residence in heaven, and Someone who could show us the way to get there.

That's how much God loves us. He gave up His beloved Son—and prepared for that agonizing moment for thousands of years. Despite this immeasurable cost, God was—and continues to be—always faithful to His promises. That is love far greater than I can comprehend.

May we live lives of gratitude in response.

LEARNING ALERT

Through Boaz's redemption of a Moabite woman—a foreigner and former idol worshipper—the Messianic chain remained unbroken. Boaz and Ruth name their son Obed, who became the father of Jesse, the father of David from whom our Messiah would be born.

The story of Ruth and Boaz is part of our spiritual heritage. From their union, our Messiah was born.

I'm getting chills right now writing this. Wow!

Praise You, Lord, for working throughout history to prepare the way for our Savior. All the energies of

Satan were directed against thwarting Your plan of redemption. But no force in heaven or hell can stand against You. You have made a way for us to be saved, to know you, and to experience complete forgiveness of our sins. In response, may we live with gratitude and faith. Amen!

Discussion Questions

1. In what ways is Boaz a blessing to Ruth? In what ways is Ruth a blessing to Boaz?

2. Describe the blessings God showers on Boaz and Ruth.

3. In what ways is Naomi a blessing to both Boaz and Ruth?

4. What blessing have you received from studying the account of Naomi, Ruth, and Boaz?

LESSON 29
David's Grandfather Is Born

Ruth 4: 16-22

> Then Naomi took the child and laid him in her lap and became his nurse. The neighbor women gave him a name, saying, "A son has been born to Naomi!" So they named him Obed. He is the father of Jesse, the father of David.
>
> Now these are the generations of Perez: to Perez was born Hezron, and to Hezron was born Ram, and to Ram, Amminadab, and to Amminadab was born Nahshon, and to Nahshon, Salmon, and to Salmon was born Boaz, and to Boaz, Obed, and to Obed was born Jesse, and to Jesse, David.
> Ruth 4: 16-22

Please don't skip this summary of Ruth!

I know genealogies are usually boring. And I know that, when reading the Bible, we usually skip right over them or, at best, skim them.

Well, Ruth ends with a genealogy, but it's a pretty cool one. First mentioned is Perez, the son of Judah: the connection between Boaz and Abraham has been established. The genealogy also states that Boaz and Ruth have a son named Obed, who fathered Jesse, who then fathered David. That's where the genealogy ends because the book of Ruth was most likely written during the time of King David.

King David is the great-grandson of Ruth and Boaz!

THE SPY

And there's more!

Another interesting fact discovered in this closing genealogy is that Salmon was the father of Boaz. According to Jewish tradition, Salmon—of the line of Judah—is possibly one of the two spies Joshua sent into Jericho to spy out the Promised Land.

When the king of Jericho discovered that spies were in his land, he sent his men to search for them. The two spies, though, had found refuge in the home of Rahab the harlot. She not only saved their lives, but she also came to embrace the God of Israel. Also, Rahab and her family were spared when Israel conquered Jericho.

Let's go with Jewish tradition and add romance to this account. So Rahab saved Salmon's life when he was on a reconnaissance mission for Joshua. This spy's appreciation turned into love, and Salmon married Rahab, the former harlot, the former idol worshipper, the Amorite foreigner. How do we know? See Matthew 1:5.

And Rahab became the mother of Boaz.

That might take a minute to sink in.

THE HARLOT

So, Boaz's mother was a foreign-born harlot—but a *redeemed* foreign-born harlot. Undoubtedly, her life and her words taught Boaz from his early years that the God of Israel is a Redeemer and that He even redeems foreigners. God gave Rahab physical protection and, more importantly, spiritual salvation. Rahab was a very special lady. She didn't do merely a good thing by hiding the two spies; she did a brave thing. Compelled by her new faith in the God of Israel, she risked her life rather than disobey this God-given opportunity to hide the spies.

Her life is so significant in God's story of redemption that she is mentioned in the Hebrews 11 hall of faith. Her name appears alongside Noah, Abraham, Moses, David, and Samuel.

And her name appears with *the harlot* still attached.

THE HEART TO REDEEM

I believe that, in most cases, Christians shouldn't carry their past sins into their new life in Christ. After all, we have been made new. Nevertheless, the Bible doesn't let us forget Rahab's past. *The harlot* sticks to her throughout the Bible. This, I believe, is to emphasize the heart of God as a Redeemer of sinful, idol-worshipping foreigners.

Yes, God chose Abraham to be the father of the nation through which He would bless the sinful world with the

Messiah. Israel is a chosen nation, but God has always had a heart for foreigners. He redeems sinners from every nation. God shows His grace to all nations.

So, Rahab retains the title of harlot throughout the Bible, not to shame her, but to highlight the heart of God. The Almighty is a Kinsman-Redeemer. Redeemer, meaning He saves and kinsman, meaning He redeems His loved ones who are lost, destitute and in desperate need.

THE UNLIKELY

Sometimes the most unlikely people find Jesus. Or—better said—Jesus finds *them*....

In 1981, I moved to Port Charlotte, Florida, to work with the youth in the community. In my first week, I met an 18-year-old named Adam. He was introduced to me as a brand-new Christian. When I learned that he had no church experience or Christian background whatsoever, I asked him how he became a Christian. He told me a most unusual account of God's amazing grace.

Adam and his best friend Frank were the ringleaders of a group of guys who were nothing but trouble. Alcohol, drugs, and rebellion were among their usual activities. They were edging toward gang involvement and considering adding guns to their collection of stolen goods.

A week before I met Adam, he and his group were smoking pot as they made plans for their evening. All of a sudden, one of them (they can't recall who it was) said, "What are we doing?"

The others looked confused.

"What are we doing with our lives?" the same person asked.

Partially buzzed, they nevertheless came to a unanimous conclusion: "Let's stop wasting our lives. Let's do something with them."

One of them said, "Let's go talk to my dad. He's a Christian, and maybe he can help us."

They walked away from their pot and went to find truth and meaning for their lives. The father shared the gospel that evening, and the guys prayed to receive Christ right then.

I met Adam that first week at my new church. Adam began to attend my youth group and Frank joined him soon after. I mentored and discipled Frank and Adam for the next three years.

As of this writing, both Frank and Adam have been pastors for nearly 25 years. In their lifetime of service to God, each of them has impacted thousands of people for eternity.

Sometimes, the most unlikely people find Jesus. Or—better said—Jesus finds them.

FOR I AM ONE

Boaz, the son of a redeemed Amorite harlot, marries a redeemed Moabite widow exactly as his father had married and redeemed Rahab, the Amorite harlot. In both cases, these women were welcomed in as family despite their sinful past and foreign roots, and both women have been honored throughout history as women of God, as women of great faith.

Boaz foreshadows our Messiah: Jesus came as our Kinsman-Redeemer, dying to pay the sin debt of not only God's chosen people, but also of the Gentile outsiders. And He welcomes all of us into the full blessings of His family.

LEARNING ALERT

Jesus' brother James shared a very important truth: *Draw near to God and He will draw near to you* (James 4:8). At a difficult time when the nation of Israel was in exile in Babylon, Jeremiah spoke to the people and said, 'For I know the plans that I have for you," declares the Lord, "plans for welfare and not for calamity to give you a future and a hope." Even when we go through pain and loss, let us remember that God is at work in our lives. Just look at the lives of Ruth and Naomi.

Praise You, God, for Your heart for sinners like me! I praise You for sending Jesus as my Kinsman-Redeemer! Amen!

Discussion Questions

1. As we complete our study of Ruth, what lesson most stands out to you? Why?

2. Having studied the book of Ruth, what do you better understand about a redeemer?

3. Psalm 149:4 says, *The Lord takes pleasure in His people; He will beautify the afflicted ones with salvation.* Explain what *beautify the afflicted ones with salvation* means in general—and what it means to you.

CHAPTER 8

ESTHER: A HEAVENLY
SCREENPLAY

LESSON 30
Introduction

If I were stranded on a desert island and you said I could only have five possessions, I would take these:

1. Blankets

2. Saw, hammer, and nails

3. Fishing pole and a bunch of hooks

4. Lots of matches

5. The book of Esther

Although you and I don't really know each other, we do have a bond, and that bond is God. You and I have committed to living a life according to His directions. We understand that we have much to be grateful for and we want to express our gratitude by obeying His Will.

So the first four items I'd take on that desert island are self-explanatory. But why the book of Esther? Good question. It's become one of my favorite books in the Bible. Actually, it's become one of my favorite books, period. Why?

Well, first of all, it's a great story. An orphan girl is raised by her cousin. She learns from him about God. She sees in him how to trust God. And she grows up to be a beautiful woman whose faith in God is extremely strong.

Theoretically having a choice of several million beautiful bachelorettes, the king of the most powerful nation in the world chooses Esther to be his queen. But there's a bad guy in the story, and evil through and through, he wants to kill all Jews. Very powerful—maybe the king's number two man—he lays a plan to have all Jews executed. But he doesn't realize Queen Esther is a Jew, which makes for good drama, as you'll see.

The narrative of Esther contains drama and suspense, some twists and turns. How would it turn out? Since you probably know this story, I don't think you need any type of spoiler-alert: good triumphs over evil.

In addition to being a great story, the book of Esther offers life lessons God wants me to carry with me even to a desert island:

1. *Prayer is powerful*, especially the prayer of a righteous person. That's why Esther calls the Jewish nation to fast and pray, and their prayers saved a nation. That's pretty impressive for an orphan girl!

2. *God has a plan for me* just as He had one for Esther before she even realized it. And God's plan is just as big for you and me as His plan for Esther was. We must be alert to how He wants to use us.

3. *God demands courage.* Following God is not for cowards. When we know His calling upon our lives and what He requires of us, we are to take action. That's our mission. What happens next is not up to us. Esther didn't know what would happen when she did what was right. She just knew she needed to act and do the right thing. She understood that her execution was a possibility, but she was obedient nevertheless.

4. *Obedience matters.* God wants me to be 100 percent in. He wants me to be fully committed to Him and willing to follow His rules regardless of my mood or the circumstances.

As we travel along Esther's journey, I think you'll see that we have a lot in common with her. And we can learn a lot from her. Although we may never be part of a royal family in the most powerful nation in the world, we do struggle to determine our calling and to be obedient... just as Esther did.

LEARNING ALERT

One other thought that we will touch on again; we must live and act in the full knowledge that Satan is alive and wants to wreak even more havoc in our lives than he already has.

These days most of us take actions to protect our families. We lock our cars, lock our houses, install security cameras and gates, and turn the alarm on before we go to sleep. What would this level of vigilance regarding the Evil One look like? What, for instance, would you do to—figuratively speaking—lock your doors?

Lord, we look forward with much anticipation to what You will teach us from this Old Testament book. Even though You're not mentioned in the text of Esther, we know You were always present just as You are always present in our lives. Even when You aren't at the forefront of our minds for much of the day, we are always Your first thought! And You are always with me! Thank You—and Amen!

LARRY SHAFFER

Discussion Questions

1. On a scale of 1 to 10, how disciplined are you in spending at least 15 minutes with God every day? Why did you give yourself that score?

2. How would your life change if you spent time every day in God's Word reading, reflecting, and writing? Be specific.

3. What do you think of the statement "Intentionally give your attention to God, or He might choose to get your attention through other means"? Is it true? Why or why not?

4. If you were going to commit to spending daily time with God, reading, reflecting, and writing, how would you go about it? Time? Place? Accountability partner? What book of the Bible? Other considerations? And what's keeping you from making this commitment?

LESSON 31
Why Study the Book of Esther

I sometimes complain about the challenge of gaining devotional insight from some of these narrative books in the Old Testament. Nevertheless, I'm drawn to Esther. But did you know that God is never mentioned in the book of Esther? Yet the reality is, we'll find God all over the book even though He is never mentioned. Hmmm, this should be interesting.

The events of Esther took place around 475 BC, making it one of the last Old Testament books to be written. Esther is a Jewish orphan who was raised by her older cousin, Mordecai, in ancient Persia.

OUR CHALLENGE

The challenge for you and me is to determine how to apply to our lives today these words written 2,500 years ago. How can what happened to a king and queen back then mean anything to us today? It's a fair question. If we have faith that God's plan includes these words in the book of Esther, then we must give this study our best effort.

I believe that by understanding a little of the circumstances surrounding this story, we can better understand God's message to you and me.

IT MIGHT HELP TO KNOW ...

The backdrop of the story of Esther is Satan's scheme to wipe out the Israelite nation. Throughout history, Satan has provided various powerful nations and individuals with aspirations to wipe the Jewish nation from the face of the earth. These haters range from the Egyptians to the Philistines to Haman (here in Esther) to Hitler.

SATAN IS SCHEMING

Satan has wielded his limited power to raise up the proverbial sword against God's chosen people in hopes of usurping God's covenants. This desire can be traced back to the curse of God on Satan in Genesis 3:15. God tells Satan that the seed of the woman he deceived will eventually crush his head. The seed of the woman is Jesus, and Satan has since attempted to disrupt or destroy the Jewish lineage that leads to Jesus. Even though Jesus has completed His redeeming work on the earth, Satan continues to inspire hatred toward the Jews because, well, he just does. He's a sore loser.

THE GAME'S NOT OVER TILL IT'S OVER

The amazing events of Esther, which we will explore in the coming days, ushered in Purim, the Jewish festival that celebrates God's sustaining the nation of Israel in Esther's time and His continual intervention to preserve His people through the ages.

You see, God never loses. He may allow the game to go to the bottom of the ninth inning, but He always manages to come up with a walk-off home run. (If you're unfamiliar with baseball, you just need to know that a walk-off home run is a dramatic way to win the game at the last minute.)

Another plot twist in Esther is that the antagonist, Haman, is an Agagite. Five hundred years earlier, God told King Saul to utterly wipe out the Agagites from the earth—and He meant *utterly* wipe them out. In that story back in I Samuel God seems very harsh. Well, Saul didn't obey God; Saul did not utterly destroy the Agagites. A remnant survived and Haman, anancestor descendant, harbored tremendous resentment toward the Jews. It's easier to understand why Haman is a true villain in Esther's story.

Lord, we look forward with much anticipation to what You will teach us in this book. Even though You're not mentioned in the text, You are always present just as You are always present in our lives. We are forever grateful that your eyes are always set upon us, and your arms never rest in bringing about what is good for our lives. *Amen!*

Discussion Questions

1. Why is it important to read the books of the Bible we might not be too familiar with?

2. Do you believe that the devil, who wreaked havoc all through the Bible, is just as eager to cause havoc in your life? Why or why not? What kind of havoc could that be?

3. Do you believe that God is just as capable of a walk-off home run for you today? Explain why or why not.

4. How do you know God is always present with you?

LESSON 32
Setting the Stage

Esther 1:1-9

> *Now it took place in the days of Ahasuerus, the Ahasuerus who reigned from India to Ethiopia over 127 provinces, in those days as King Ahasuerus sat on his royal throne which was at the citadel in Susa, in the third year of his reign he gave a banquet for all his princes and attendants, the army officers of Persia and Media, the nobles and the princes of his provinces being in his presence. And he displayed the riches of his royal glory and the splendor of his great majesty for many days, 180 days.*

> *When these days were completed, the king gave a banquet lasting seven days for all the people who were present at the citadel in Susa, from the greatest to the least, in the court of the garden of the king's palace. There were hangings of fine white and violet linen held by cords of fine purple linen on silver rings and marble columns, and couches of gold and silver on a mosaic pavement of porphyry, marble, mother-of-pearl and precious stones. Drinks were served in golden vessels of various kinds, and the royal wine was plentiful according to the king's bounty. The drinking was done according to the law, there was no compulsion, for so the king had given orders to each official of his household that he should do according to the desires of each person. Queen*

> *Vashti also gave a banquet for the women in the palace which belonged to King Ahasuerus.*
> Esther 1: 1-9 (NASB)

IT MIGHT HELP TO KNOW ...

The story takes place in ancient Persia when that nation is the reigning world empire. Nearly 50 million people reside in the empire during the early 400s BC. Persia had conquered Babylon many years earlier (539 BC), so the Jews residing in Babylon—the descendants of the one-time-captive Jews—are now part of the Persian empire.

Esther is a young orphan during the time of King Darius, well-known for his battles with the Greeks who would eventually defeat Persia under Alexander the Great. One of the famous battles between Darius and the Greeks is the battle of Marathon in 490 BC where, although the Persians are favored, Darius suffers defeat.

Enraged, he vows revenge but dies shortly thereafter before he could mount another attack. Darius's son, Xerxes, takes over as king and vows to carry out his father's revenge. Xerxes battles the Greeks repeatedly. He has some successes and some defeats, and eventually the Greeks prevail.

THE KING WITH TWO NAMES

All this to say, Esther is born late in the reign of Darius and comes of age during the reign of his son, Xerxes. And *Xerxes* is the name the Greeks gave him; the Hebrews call him

Ahasuerus. Xerxes/Ahasuerus is the king who eventually takes Esther as his bride.

We read that *in the third year of his reign he gave a banquet... and he displayed the riches of his royal glory and the splendor of his great majesty for many days, 180 days.*

Clearly, this new king has inherited great wealth He can do anything he wants, have anything he wants, and go anywhere he wants. He is always ready to party.

Most likely, however, Xerxes/Ahasuerus calls his men together to plan out military campaigns and strategies that will enable them to utterly defeat the Greeks. As the Hebrew writer tells us, the strategy meetings end with a seven-day banquet. Wine and food take center stage.

THE KING OF THE WORLD

The drama begins with Ahasuerus (again, this is the Hebrew name of Xerxes) assuming the role of "king of the world." Did you notice no mention of God? Some things never change. World rulers have always thought of themselves as men of ultimate power and not given any thought to God. Little does Ahasuerus realize that the unseen God is orchestrating the entire scene for His divine purposes. Ahasuerus is simply a play actor in the drama that God is writing and producing. In the next scene, God is going to really rock this king's world with the defiance of his current wife Vashti.

LEARNING ALERT

At times in my life I could not see God; I was in the valley. Where was God?

As we see in this text, just because we feel alone doesn't mean we *are* alone! God is with us in the green pastures and in the shadow of death (Psalm 23). Our loving God is not only with us, but He is also working on our behalf in ways we may never know this side of heaven.

How then should we live? With trust. Choosing to believe that God provides the perfect trifecta in our lives.

1. He loves us and wants the best for us. This is omni-love.

2. He is supremely wise and knows what is best for us. This is omniscience.

3. He is all-powerful and can bring about what is best for us. This is omnipotence.

God loves us, He is wise, and He is all-powerful. Now that is the perfect one, two, three punch. (I took the liberty of adding that third punch!) God is real. We are not alone. He has great plans for us. We must have the courage to trust Him even when we walk through life's valleys.

Lord, in the coming days, teach us more about You and Your divine providence in our lives. Help us avoid the sin of living this life as if it is our own. We are Yours. May we be mindful of You, obedient to Your ways, and fed by Your Word, always. Amen!

Discussion Questions

1. What does it mean to be actively conscious of God throughout the day? What can you do to grow in your awareness of God? Be specific and practical.

2. Consider further the trifecta of God. What does it mean to you that God loves you, is wise, and is all-powerful? In what ways could these truths change the way you live? Again, be specific.

3. How do you feel about the following statement: God directs the powerful energy of His attributes directly toward you personally?

LESSON 33
Vashti's Rebellion

Esther 1:10-12, 19-21

> *On the seventh day, when the heart of the king was merry with wine, he commanded Mehuman, Biztha, Harbona, Bigtha, Abagtha, Zethar and Carkas, the seven eunuchs who served in the presence of King Ahasuerus, to bring Queen Vashti before the king with her royal crown in order to display her beauty to the people and the princes, for she was beautiful. But Queen Vashti refused to come at the king's command delivered by the eunuchs. Then the king became very angry and his wrath burned within him.*
> Esther 1:10-12

THE UNSEEN GOD REIGNS

The story begins with a pagan king who appears to be the main character of the story. The Hebrew writer chooses to *not* include God in the story. This is a departure from the typical Old Testament narratives, but it's clearly an intentional and effective technique. The narrative clearly conveys the way the world views God or should I say *doesn't* view God.

Many people live without much thought of God. I think that's especially true of people in positions of great power, such as the king in our story. They get up in the morning and go through the day without considering the purposes of God, the providence of God, or the uniqueness of His people. They are consumed with their world, their purpose, and their own uniqueness.

So why is the book of Esther in the Bible if it doesn't even mention God? History has repeatedly confirmed that the book of Esther is canonical: it belongs in the Bible. Furthermore, the story is so brilliantly written that the work of God, especially His providence, is all over the events described. King Ahasuerus believes he is sovereign when, in reality, he is only a puppet.

LET'S PARTY!

Chapter 1 sets up the story. In order for God to place the right person in the presence of the king to influence a pivotal decision in the near future, He needed to have the current queen removed from her position. So, during the extended banquet, *on the seventh day, when the heart of the king was merry with wine, he commanded... Queen Vashti [to come] before the king with her royal crown in order to display her beauty to the people and the princes, for she was beautiful* (verses 10-11).

The text doesn't tell us why, although we can certainly guess, but the queen sends back word that she is not coming to the king's drunk fest. She decides, that his banquet hall is no place for a dignified woman. It could also reasonably be speculated that the king wants her to wear her crown—and only her crown. She says no. And her no sends the king into a rage. A real buzzkill for the party.

WOMEN RULE, MEN DROOL

The king gathers his council of seven princes and asks them what he should do. The council, fearing that their wives will follow Vashti's example, advise that he write a decree declaring that wives should honor their husbands to keep order in the kingdom. Apparently, they fear an uprising from their wives. The king writes the decree and removes Vashti from her position as queen.

HOW FOOLISH

The king and his council work hard to control the situation. We humans feel we can orchestrate our lives to bring about our own desired results without seeking the counsel of God. How foolish! How often do we fall into that same trap?

About 500 years later, Jesus talks about the importance of being poor in spirit. He does not mean having little spirit. He means that to truly be fulfilled in life, we must recognize our need for God. We are poverty stricken without Him, and it is only because of His grace that we obtain citizenship in heaven.

When Jesus says these words, He knows that the grace will be made possible through His sacrificial death. Jesus pays the debt we can't pay, and in response we should acknowledge our need and be grateful. How do we show our gratitude? We live in obedience and humility before God, and we love and serve the people we come in contact with.

LEARNING ALERT

I first memorized Philippians 4:6-7 when I was a senior in high school:

> *Be anxious for nothing, but in everything by prayer and supplication with thanksgiving let your requests be made known to God. And the peace of God, which surpasses all comprehension, will guard your hearts and your minds in Christ Jesus.*

I clearly remember the first time I consciously realized the truth of this verse. I was in college and stressed out about something. I remember being especially worried about possible negative outcomes that might come my way. So I decided to go for a run.

As the reasons for stress rolled through my brain, I suddenly realized that I hadn't prayed. The verse I had memorized a year earlier came to mind. I prayed and turned that stress all over to God. After my prayer, a peace came over me that stopped me in my tracks. It was an amazing sense of calm and the presence of God. Why did I wait so long to simply pray and turn my worries over to God?

Throughout history men and women have gotten into trouble when they depended on their own wisdom. You and I can say the same about our lives, can't we? Just as the devil convinced Adam and Eve that they knew more than God, the devil is trying to do the same thing with you and me. God tells us to seek His counsel as we navigate our episodes of life. I challenge you to join me in asking for God's direction each day.

We praise You, God that, because Your Word is living and active, Your truth influences our character and our life. Keep us turning to You often for guidance and wisdom. May our consciousness be filled with You. May we look at every circumstance through Your eyes and from Your point of view. We praise You, for You are God! Amen!

Discussion Questions

1. What steps do you take to seek God's counsel?

2. When is the last time you sought God's counsel? What was the result?

3. Briefly tell of a time you should have sought God's counsel and didn't. What happened? What might have been different if you'd sought God's counsel?

4. How can you be sure that your decisions are in line with God's will?

LESSON 34
The Search for a New Queen

Esther 2:1-4

> *After these things, when the anger of King Ahasuerus had subsided, he remembered Vashti and what she had done and what had been decreed against her. Then the king's attendants, who served him, said, "Let beautiful young virgins be sought for the king. Let the king appoint overseers in all the provinces of his kingdom that they may gather every beautiful young virgin to the citadel of Susa, to the harem, into the custody of Hegai, the king's eunuch, who is in charge of the women; and let their cosmetics be given them. Then let the young lady who pleases the king be queen in place of Vashti." And the matter pleased the king, and he did accordingly.*
> Esther 2:1-4

THE BEAUTY PAGEANT

After the embarrassment of the banquet and his subsequent decree requiring women to submit, the king most likely diverts his attention and engages in warfare with the Greeks. But eventually his mind returns to his need for love.

At some point he goes back to the palace, and the sting of missing Vashti hits him. His anger has subsided, but he can't reconcile with her because of his decree. His servants, seeing his state, suggest, "*Let beautiful young virgins be sought for the king...then let the young lady who pleases the king be queen in Vashti's place. And the matter pleased the king and he did accordingly"* (vs. 2-4). I suppose a beauty pageant was just what the king needed to get over his lovely queen.

The Bachelor

What we have here is the first episode of the TV reality show *The Bachelor*....

Auditions for several million women in the Persian kingdom are organized throughout the land. The goal is to find the most beautiful virgins in the land. Most likely poise, demeanor, and reputation are considered as well. The chosen women will be escorted to the palace for a 12-month beautification process with six months with oil and myrrh and then six months spices and cosmetics. (I assume, of course, all were organic and non-toxic. Essential oils, of course, were all the rage.)

After this 12-month spa treatment, the women are taken to the king, and he will ultimately choose the one who pleases him. Yes, that is the ultimate *The Bachelor* show! With millions of competitors, how does God orchestrate Esther to be the king's choice? Well, He is God, and He's done much bigger things. Bottom line, God wants Esther in place to do His work.

LEARNING ALERT

One advantage of old age is being able to look back over our lives and recognize God's providence in certain key circumstances. I couldn't see His hand as events unfolded. I was simply living my life with little thought of the future. But now, looking back, I see pretty clearly His involvement.

Certain people—especially my wife, but a few other dear people as well—have played key roles in shaping my character and my life. When I look back at the seemingly random ways that certain people crossed my path 30 to 40 years ago, I now clearly see the hand of God.

Just as God's will was accomplished in the Persian kingdom, it is still being accomplished today. God works in all situations, in all stages of life, and in all countries. We must have the faith to believe that we can ask Him for help wherever we are and whenever we need Him. We must also believe that He uses us for His purposes.

Lord, we wonder how often You have orchestrated our lives to place us in positions to do Your work. How often are we faithful—and how often do we miss or resist the opportunity? I'm afraid to really know the answer to that question. May we be more mindful and aware of the opportunities you give us, whether big or small, and may we be faithful to act. Amen!

Discussion Questions

1. Is it ever hard for you to trust God? Why?

2. When have you struggled to trust God because people who don't trust Him seem to be doing better than you? What truth(s) do you tell yourself when these thoughts hit?

3. What do you do to fight feeling insignificant?

LESSON 35
Esther Becomes a Candidate

Esther 2:8-11, 13–16

> So it came about when the command and decree of the
> king were heard and many young ladies were gathered
> to the citadel of Susa into the custody of Hegai, that
> Esther was taken to the king's palace into the custody of
> Hegai, who was in charge of the women. Now the young
> lady pleased him and found favor with him.
>
> So he quickly provided her with her cosmetics and food,
> gave her seven choice maids from the king's palace and
> transferred her and her maids to the best place in the
> harem. Esther did not make known her people or her
> kindred, for Mordecai had instructed her that she should
> not make them known. Every day Mordecai walked back
> and forth in front of the court of the harem to learn how
> Esther was and how she fared....
>
> The young lady would go into the king in this way:
> anything that she desired was given her to take with her
> from the harem to the king's palace. In the evening she
> would go in and, in the morning, she would return to
> the second harem, to the custody of Shaashgaz, the king's
> eunuch who was in charge of the concubines. She would
> not again go into the king unless the king delighted in
> her and she was summoned by name.
>
> Now when the turn of Esther, the daughter of Abihail the
> uncle of Mordecai who had taken her as his daughter,

> *came to go into the king, she did not request anything*
> *except what Hegai, the king's eunuch who was in charge*
> *of the women, advised. And Esther found favor in the*
> *eyes of all who saw her. So Esther was taken to King*
> *Ahasuerus to his royal palace in the tenth month which*
> *is the month Tebeth, in the seventh year of his reign.*
> Esther 2:8-11, 13–16

The king wants a new queen, so an epic beauty contest is under way. Chosen women from all over the massive Persian empire are brought to the palace. Each one of them goes through a 12-month beautification process using oils and spices. After the 12 months, "the young lady would go into the king in this way: anything she desired was given her to take with her from the harem to the king's palace" (verse 13).

I have no idea the kind of things they would choose to take, but the women are to creatively add to their appeal. Verse 14 continues: "In the evening [the woman] would go in and, in the morning, she would return to the second harem, to the custody of Shaashgaz... She would not again go into the king unless the king delighted in her and she was summoned by name."

YOU'RE NEXT

Now it's Esther's turn. The Jewish orphan is about to go before the king. The most beautiful women in the empire have gone before her. Verse 15 (emphasis added) says, *Now when the turn of Esther... came to go into the king, she did not request anything except what was advised. And Esther found favor in the eyes of all who saw her.* Esther was taken to king Ahasuerus.

What is it about Esther? An orphan from humble means captures the hearts of everyone she meets. We know she must have been stunningly beautiful, but there must be something else about her if she stands out among the hottest supermodels of the Persian empire.

Clearly, beauty is not the determining factor that makes Esther unique. Everyone notices that Esther is different from all the others. God grants her favor in the eyes of all who meet her. There must be something about her demeanor, her kindness, her humility, her spirit, her warmth, her sense of humor, her charm, her face, and, her eyes.

God fashioned this special young woman inside her mother's womb. During her childhood and adolescence, He grew in her a natural beauty rooted deep in her heart. God did all this because He had a plan and a purpose.

SOMETHING IN THE WAY SHE MOVES

I grew up listening to the Beatles. My older brother had every album. One of their songs was "Something":

Something in the way she moves,
attracts me like no other lover...
Something in her style that shows me,
I don't want to leave her now.

It seems everyone who encounters Esther loves her. But what about the king? The writer gets right to the point. Verse 17 says, "The king loved Esther more than all the women, and she found favor and kindness with him more than all the virgins, so that he set the royal crown on her head and made her queen instead of Vashti."

These words suggest that Esther's appeal went beyond her physical beauty. The king loves her. Something about her makes him want to give favor and kindness to her. The reigning king of the world's greatest empire, who is occupied with his own desires and achievements, extends humble care, kindness, and benevolence to this woman with no money and no family.

Wow, Esther is special! She is something! And in the providence of God, He has fashioned her as such for a unique purpose and a time that is yet to come. *The king thinks he is making his own choice, but we know better. How naïve he is!* God is orchestrating something amazing!

LEARNING ALERT

God has made each of us unique. Chances are, we aren't as beautiful as Esther. Chances are we won't find favor with everyone we meet. But each of us can be absolutely confident that God cares just as much about us as He did about Esther. That's an important truth.

Not convinced? Let me remind you that God knows your name. He knows the number of hairs on your head. He understands your joys and your heartbreaks. And He loves you so much that He made the biggest sacrifice He could make so you could avoid the horrific consequences of hell and instead live with Him forever. When you understand God's love for you, you can rest in the security that He is at work in you *to will and to work for His good pleasure* (Philippians 2:13).

Yes, the uniqueness of Esther was God's favor in her life, but He had shown His favor earlier, developing her character and growing in her integrity, courage, purity, and kindness. It should be the same for us.

In addition to unique gifts and personalities, we each walk a unique path that brings us into contact with certain people, and we make impressions on the people we meet. Sometimes our experiences bring us in contact with the rich, famous, and powerful people of the world. Sometimes our experiences bring us before the lowly and hurting. In either case, we are to be honest, to be kind, and to serve as Jesus would. God favors the faithful and loving.

Every day as we walk along our unique paths, we encounter regular people going through life in the usual manner. Are we mindful of why God has our paths cross? In those seemingly ordinary moments, are we asking God to use our lives and our words for His purposes? You never know when God wants to use you. Always be prepared and alert.

Lord, help us to live out and apply these principles in our lives. By Your power and grace, sow seeds of kindness, righteousness, and goodness in our hearts. Help us to act as Your ambassadors in this world and to honor You by being servants You can use. Amen!

Discussion Questions

1. Often the world speaks of self-esteem. As a Christian, what is the Christian equivalent? What do you think is an accurate way to view yourself?

2. Do you believe that God causes us to come into contact with certain people? Why or why not? If so, what new perspective on daily life does that give you?

3. What does it mean that you are *fearfully and wonderfully made* (Psalm 139:14)?

4. In what ways, if any, do you identify with Esther? Be specific.

LESSON 36
An Assassination Foiled!

Esther 2:21 – 3:6

In those days, while Mordecai was sitting at the king's gate, Bigthan and Teresh, two of the king's officials from those who guarded the door, became angry and sought to lay hands on King Ahasuerus. But the plot became known to Mordecai and he told Queen Esther, and Esther informed the king in Mordecai's name. Now when the plot was investigated and found to be so, they were both hanged on gallows; and it was written in the Book of the Chronicles in the king's presence.

After these events King Ahasuerus promoted Haman, the son of Hammedatha the Agagite, and advanced him and established his authority over all the princes who were with him. All the king's servants who were at the king's gate bowed down and paid homage to Haman; for so the king had commanded concerning him. But Mordecai neither bowed down nor paid homage. Then the king's servants who were at the king's gate said to Mordecai, "Why are you transgressing the king's command?" Now it was when they had spoken daily to him and he would not listen to them, that they told Haman to see whether Mordecai's reason would stand; for he had told them that he was a Jew. When Haman saw that Mordecai neither bowed down nor paid homage to him, Haman was filled with rage. But he disdained to lay hands on Mordecai alone, for they

had told him who the people of Mordecai were; therefore Haman sought to destroy all the Jews, the people of Mordecai, who were throughout the whole kingdom of Ahasuerus.
Esther 2:21 – 3:6

MORDECAI AND HAMAN

King Ahasuerus loves Esther. By God's providence, the king is absolutely smitten; it was love at first sight. Esther has rocked his world, so the king declares a holiday and holds a massive banquet to celebrate his new bride.

This text reminds us, though, that throughout this Cinderella-like fairytale time, Esther keeps her nationality unknown exactly as her cousin Mordecai had instructed her.

THE PLOT IS SPOILED

Meanwhile, Mordecai sits at the front gate of the palace to stay as close to Esther as possible. We don't know any further details. What does *sit at the gate* mean? I'd like to know. But regardless of the sacrifice and perhaps humble situation, he did it out of his loyal fatherly love for Esther. She sits on the throne, and he sits at the gate. God's plan is unfolding....

While sitting at the gate one day, Mordecai hears of a plot against the king's life:

The plot became known to Mordecai and he told Queen Esther, and Esther informed the king in Mordecai's name. Now when the plot was investigated and found to be so,

they were both hanged on the gallows; and it was written
in the Book of the Chronicles in the king's presence.
Esther 2:22

God will use this important event in a most extraordinary
way. Stay tuned!

HERE COMES THE BAD GUY

At some point after these events, the king promotes a man
named Haman to a high position in the court. Haman is now
responsible for overseeing many princes and provinces—
and this is a very big deal.

Now, it's important to remember that Haman is a
descendant of Agag, and the Agagites hated the Jews,
especially the line of Saul. Mordecai is, of course, a
descendant of.... guess who? Saul.

The plot thickens as the king commands all in his empire
to bow and pay homage to Haman in his new and exalted
position. Mordecai will have none of it. He refuses to bow
and pay homage.

The king's servants at the gate, hoping to avoid conflict,
urge Mordecai to bow. Mordecai refuses, stating that he is
a Jew who absolutely will not bow to an Agagite. The racial
disdain is thick on both sides.

After many days of urging Mordecai to bow, and his
refusing to, the king's servants inform Haman—who is
enraged. But, according to verse 6, Haman chooses not

to *lay hands on Mordecai alone, for they told him who the people of Mordecai were; therefore, Haman sought to destroy all Jews, the people of Mordecai, who were throughout the whole kingdom of Ahasuerus* (verse 6). Haman holds back his revenge on Mordecai to consider how to destroy all the Jews. More on this next time.

LEARNING ALERT

Let's keep considering how God providentially uses us in our daily lives to reach, touch, and impact others. We never know exactly whom He is going to bring into our lives. But we know that we are best used by Him when we stand firm in our biblical convictions and live with moral courage according to godly principles. Mordecai is quite an example of fortified resolve and moral courage. He determines to do what was right, whatever the consequences.

On a much smaller scale, I had a similar experience. I knew my fifth-grade teacher was very eager to teach us the principles of Darwinian evolution. By that time, I had spent a few years in Baptist Sunday school. I believed in creation, and I knew in my heart that the principles of evolution did not align with my Bible. I don't know where I got the resolve, but I asked to be excused from the lessons on evolution because of my religious beliefs. I was allowed to sit way in the back, at my own table, with my back turned to the class, and doing my own work. I endured some ridicule, but I remember that, in my mind, I was just doing what I thought was the right thing to do. Period.

We who love Jesus simply have to be faithful to God each day, even when the situation is uncomfortable, and the odds are against us. In due time, God will grant His favor, sometimes in the most wonderful and unexpected ways. Galatians 6:9 says, *Let us not grow weary of doing good, for in due season we will reap, if we do not give up.*

Another guiding verse from the apostle Paul in 2 Timothy 2 where he calls us to cleanse ourselves and live righteously according to God's Word. When we do so, Paul wrote, we will be a *vessel for honor, sanctified, useful to the Master, prepared for every good work"* (verse 21). Amen!

Discussion Questions

1. What does it mean to be a *vessel for honor* (2 Timothy 2:21)?

2. Why do you think we should be *prepared for every good work?* (verse 21)

3. 3. Describe a time when you or someone you know exhibited moral courage. What was the reaction of witnesses?

LESSON 37
Haman's Plot

Esther 3: 8–11

> *Then Haman said to King Ahasuerus, "There is a certain people scattered and dispersed among the peoples in all the provinces of your kingdom; their laws are different from those of all other people and they do not observe the king's laws, so it is not in the king's interest to let them remain. If it is pleasing to the king, let it be decreed that they be destroyed, and I will pay ten thousand talents of silver into the hands of those who carry on the king's business, to put into the king's treasuries."*

> *Then the king took his signet ring from his hand and gave it to Haman, the son of Hammedatha the Agagite, the enemy of the Jews. The king said to Haman, "The silver is yours, and the people also, to do with them as you please."*
> Esther 3:8–11

THE PLOT

Here's what's happened so far.... The ruler of Persia—the world's largest empire at this time—was King Ahasuerus. Approximately 40 million people lived in the empire, including many Jews who had previously been victims of the Babylonian captivity. Queen Vashti defied the king publicly, and he removed her as queen.

To find the king a new queen, an empire wide beauty contest was arranged. The most beautiful virgins were brought to the palace for the first episode ever of the reality TV show *The Bachelor*. Esther, a Jewish orphan raised by her older cousin Mordecai swept the king off his feet with her beauty, poise, and irresistible presence. She did not reveal that she was a Jew.

Meanwhile, at the palace gate, Mordecai hears of a plot to kill the king. He alerts Esther who tells the king. The investigation proves Mordecai to be correct. The conspirators are hung, and Mordecai's actions are recorded in the king's book of records.

After these events, Haman, an Agagite, is promoted by the king to rule over many provinces. When Haman passes by, the people are to bow before him, but Mordecai refuses to bow: the Agagites are ancient enemies of Israel. Haman is enraged at Mordecai's defiance, but instead of singling out Mordecai for punishment, Haman devises a plot to take out all the Jews in the empire.

As I've said, God is never mentioned in the book of Esther, but the primary theme that clearly emerges is the amazing providence of God.

TIMING IS EVERYTHING

At the right time, Haman approaches the king with a plan:

> *There are a certain people scattered and dispersed among the peoples in all the provinces of your kingdom;*

their laws are different from those of all other people and
they do not observe the king's laws.
Esther 3:8

Note that Haman doesn't identify that *certain people* as Jews, and the king doesn't bother to ask for specifics.

Haman continues: *It is not in the king's interest to let them remain. If it is pleasing to the king, let it be decreed that they be destroyed* (verses 8-9). The king gives Haman his signet ring, indicating that Haman can decree whatever he wants. Haman has ultimate power to do as he pleases. He secures funds and organizes the provinces to carry out genocide against the Israelites on a set day. Haman's plan is coming together beautifully. He must be feeling extremely proud and, oh, so brilliant!

TAKING ACTION

When certain human beings carry out their own selfish agenda, the account is characterized by action, intent, and power. They plot, they plan, they reason, they organize because they believe that they are bringing about their desired ends. They live in this world as if the events of life are a combination of randomness, chance, and their own efforts.

They seek to gain control by making things happen. Their creed is "You are the captain of your own ship."

So why would the author of Esther not mention God? Most people—then and now live as if God doesn't exist. The people approach each day pursuing a sense of control by exerting their own actions toward their desired ends—and they often do all this apart from and unaware of God.

We human beings are no different today. The average person lives each day without even a passing thought of Colossians 3:1-2:

> If you have been raised up with Christ, keep seeking the things above, where Christ is, seated at the right hand of God. Set your mind on the things above, not the things that are on earth.

LEARNING ALERT

As Christians, we can find it challenging to balance our daily responsibilities with the understanding of God's providence and sovereign control? We are Christians, but we still yearn to have control. What is the right balance—or is it a balance at all? We'll explore this question further as we work our way through Esther.

Now, I'm going to share a story of when I left God out of a serious situation, I was dealing with during a mission trip to Africa. This trip was my third to Malawi, a country in the southeastern part of the continent, and I flew out of Houston on July 31, 2013. I would be flying from Houston… to Amsterdam… to Nairobi, Kenya… and finally to Lilongwe, Malawi, with a brief scheduled stopover in Lusaka, Zambia. Not exactly a direct flight. The flights were long but fairly uneventful… until we were only a few hundred miles from Malawi. Then the adventure began.

My Kenya Airlines plane was about to touch down in Lusaka, Zambia, for a one-hour layover when suddenly it pulled up, accelerating back into full flight. The pilot announced with a rather monotone voice that he had to pull up because of a flap malfunction. We would circle the airport during the troubleshooting. The announcement ended.

I BEGIN TO PROCESS

A flap malfunction!!!! Hmmmm.

No problem! They'll do some troubleshooting. After all, how important can a flap be?

Throughout the next 15 dreadful minutes of circling Lusaka, Zambia, I focused on my love for my wife, children, and grandchildren. I wondered about the current state of my life insurance and will. And of course I pondered my regrets and failures and even a few accomplishments.

I thought about my loving relationships and a few broken relationships. *Did I tell my loved ones often enough that I love them?* Then, after about 15 minutes, I finally got around to considering God in all this. I recalled His sovereignty and remembered I can rest in His complete control of the situation. Nothing is random. If it's time for me to go, then so be it. If not, so be it. Perhaps I should let the *peace of God, which surpasses all understanding* take control (Philippians 4:7 ESV).

Just then, after 15 minutes of fear and worry and a few sweet seconds of experiencing God's peace, the pilot announced that the situation had been resolved and we landed without incident.

Whew! And what a lesson for me! In the last few seconds of those 15 minutes of terror, I finally got to the thoughts of the sovereignty of God in all things and experienced His peace…. Just in time!!!

In that life-and-death situation, my faith in God's sovereignty was real. (It's our secret that it took 15 long minutes of utter terror to get me there). I'm glad to be able to say that I finally did indeed pull God into the harrowing equation. After all, I was on a mission trip.

Lord, teach us to live very aware of Your presence with us. Keep us prayerful, always asking for Your guidance and then always following it. Amen!

Discussion Questions

1. Define God's providence both broadly and personally.

2. Tell of a time you've seen God's providence in your life. What did that experience do to your faith and/or your relationship with God?

3. Why is it important for us to recognize God's sovereign control? What blessings come with that recognition?

4. What is your personal responsibility to secure desirable outcomes? Perhaps give an example. Strive to be specific.

LESSON 38
Haman's Hideous Plan

Esther 4:1-3, 8-13

When Mordecai learned all that had been done, he tore his clothes, put on sackcloth and ashes, and went out into the midst of the city and wailed loudly and bitterly. He went as far as the king's gate, for no one was to enter the king's gate clothed in sackcloth. In each and every province where the command and decree of the king came, there was great mourning among the Jews, with fasting, weeping and wailing; and many lay on sackcloth and ashes....

[Mordecai] also gave [the king's servant Hathach] a copy of the text of the edict which had been issued in Susa for their destruction, that he might show Esther and inform her, and to order her to go in to the king to implore his favor and to plead with him for her people.

Hathach came back and related Mordecai's words to Esther. Then Esther spoke to Hathach and ordered him to reply to Mordecai: "All the king's servants and the people of the king's provinces know that for any man or woman who comes to the king to the inner court who is not summoned, he has but one law, that he be put to death, unless the king holds out to him the golden scepter so that he may live. And I have not been summoned to come to the king for these thirty days." They related Esther's words to Mordecai.

> *Then Mordecai told them to reply to Esther, "Do not imagine that you in the king's palace can escape any more than all the Jews."*
> Esther 4:1-3, 8-13

IT'S SHOWTIME!

Haman has gained consent, authority, and funding to carry out his plan to exterminate all Jews living in the Persian Empire. The edict has been distributed, and the provinces are preparing to carry out the gruesome act. When Mordecai learns of the edict, he weeps and wails bitterly. In each province there is great mourning, fasting, and weeping among the Jews.

HAVE I LOST FAVOR?

When Esther hears about the edict, she sends a messenger to Mordecai to learn what and why this event occurred. Mordecai tells the messenger what happened and gives him a copy of the edict to show Esther. Mordecai commands Esther to go to the king to implore his favor and to plead with him for the people of Israel.

When Esther receives word back, she agonizes over the reality that any person who goes before the king without being summoned can be put to death. If the king does not extend his golden scepter toward the person approaching, that individual would die. Esther's fear and uncertainty are especially high because he hasn't summoned her in 30 days. Perhaps she has lost favor with him?

THE TIME IS NOW

Mordecai hears back regarding Esther's concerns. With great wisdom and clarity, Mordecai summarizes the situation by saying the following:

> *Do not imagine that you in the king's palace can escape any more than all the Jews. For if you remain silent at this time, relief and deliverance will arise for the Jews from another place and you and your father's house will perish. And who knows whether you have not attained royalty* for such a time as this."
> Esther 4:13-14, emphasis added

This is, I believe, the most important statement in the book.

Esther responds to Mordecai with a request that he have the Jews pray and fast. She also courageously declares, *I will go to the king, which is not according to the law; and if I perish, I perish"* (verse 16).

Without mentioning God or prayer, the author of Esther has nevertheless presented an appropriate view of God, His sovereignty, and the certain fulfillment of His purposes. Acknowledging that her life is in God's hands, Esther commits to doing what is right: she submits to God, knowing that whatever He wants to happen will happen.

A FEW OBSERVATIONS

Mordecai knows that God will not allow all the Jews to perish because Mordecai knows the covenant promises God made to Abraham and David, and Mordecai is confident that God will keep His promises. Mordecai knows that God will make Israel a great nation and that, from the seed of David, the Messiah would someday come. This man of faith also knows that God will protect a remnant of His people in order to ensure the Messianic line, but he doesn't know how many Jewish casualties would result. Mordecai finds the possibility that many people could be murdered absolutely horrific.

Upon hearing of the edict, Mordecai immediately knows that Esther has the best opportunity to save the greatest number of God's people. Mordecai also sees at least some of the reason and purpose behind the events of Esther's life that led her to the palace. Her journey wasn't a matter of random good fortune. The events occurred for a reason. For God's reasons. Esther's beauty, grace, and winsomeness were all gifts from God. All that had happened to Esther was—as Mordecai told her—*for such a time as this* (verse 14).

LEARNING ALERT

Esther's initial response is not prompted by selfishness. Her head is undoubtedly spinning, and she's trying to process the situation. Upon hearing Mordecai's reminder that she may not be spared and that God will protect His people some other way if she doesn't step up, Esther chooses to have the same confidence in God's power and purpose that Mordecai does. She resolves to go before the king as a servant of God and leave the results to Him.

And notice what she did and what she encouraged others to do before she acted: Esther fasts and prays. We cannot overestimate the power of prayer! My finite, human brain cannot fully comprehend that, anytime and from anywhere, I have access to the God of Esther and the Creator of the universe!

If you're like me, you hear a lot of prayer requests at church, in the church bulletin, in church emails, from family, and from friends. Too often I wonder if my one more prayer will make any difference at all. But that thought is contrary to the Lord's instructions to us. He calls us to pray for others, whether we are one of a few people praying or one of millions.

Bottom line, God invites us to talk to Him, and He has specifically told us that He wants us to pray for others. Think about how the men and women of the Bible prayed to God, and they did so with heartfelt sincerity and faith. Think, too, about how often Jesus Himself prayed.

Lord, may we be mindful of the opportunities You have given us. You don't need us, per se, because You will accomplish Your purposes with or without us. But You kindly do want to use us, and we are blessed accordingly. We are honored to be Your servants. May we act as such and not consider our good fortunes as something we deserve but as something we can use for Your purposes and Your glory. Amen!

Discussion Questions

1. Identify several situations when Christians today have to stand up for what's right.

2. In light of those realities, how does the idea of being prepared "for such a time as this" apply to you?

3. What do you do to decide whether to take action or to let God bring an outcome?

LESSON 39
Laying the Trap

Esther 5:5-11

*The king said, "Bring Haman quickly that we may do as
Esther desires." So the king and Haman came to the
banquet which Esther had prepared. As they drank their
wine at the banquet, the king said to Esther, "What is
your petition, for it shall be granted to you. And what
is your request? Even to half of the kingdom it shall be
done." So Esther replied, "My petition and my request
is: if I have found favor in the sight of the king, and if
it pleases the king to grant my petition and do what I
request, may the king and Haman come to the banquet
which I will prepare for them, and tomorrow I will do as
the king says."*

*Then Haman went out that day glad and pleased of
heart; but when Haman saw Mordecai in the king's gate
and that he did not stand up or tremble before him,
Haman was filled with anger against Mordecai. Haman
controlled himself, however, went to his house and sent for
his friends and his wife Zeresh. Then Haman recounted
to them the glory of his riches, and the number of his
sons, and every instance where the king had magnified
him and how he had promoted him above the princes
and servants of the king.*
Esther 5:5-11

FLEETING GLORY AND RICHES

Esther has settled in her mind that God had made her queen specifically for the task at hand. Having determined to go before the king and plead for her people, Esther doesn't wait long. After three days of fasting, she puts on her royal robes and stands in the inner court in front of the king's rooms.

Has she lost favor with the king?

Was this fairytale about to end in tragedy?

Esther 5:2 answers those questions:

When the king saw Esther the queen standing in the court, she obtained favor in his sight; and the king extended to Esther the golden scepter...then the king said to her," 'What is troubling you, Queen Esther? What is your request? Even to half the kingdom it shall be given you."

While her heart pounds in trepidation, his apparently pounds in delight at seeing her. So delighted by her presence, the king is willing to grant Esther whatever she wants, up to half the kingdom. Unbelievable!

ESTHER'S STRATEGY

The king wants to know what's troubling Esther. What should she say and how should she say it?" Having thought about this encounter and prayed about her assignment, Esther acts with great wisdom: she chooses to provide the king with context before she makes her real request. So she asks if the king would come and bring Haman to a banquet she has prepared for them. Delighted, the king calls for Haman.

Now, we don't know if God prompted Esther to proceed with this plan during her time of fasting and prayer. Or maybe He gave her this idea as she stood before the king—or perhaps just minutes earlier. We do not know, and the timing doesn't matter. What does matter is Esther's sensitivity to God's presence in her life, her mind, and her heart.

At the banquet, the king again asks Esther for her request, again reaffirming she could have anything, even half the kingdom. But rather than answering directly, she asks that the king and Haman attend one more banquet the next day, and she promises that she will make her request then.

What a strategist! Glad to have more time with Esther, the king agrees.

PRIDE

Bursting with pride, a very happy Haman leaves the banquet and heads home. On the way he sees Mordecai, who *did not stand up or tremble before him* as others did (verse 9).

Filled with anger, Haman manages to control himself, makes it home, and appeases his rage by calling together his wife and friends to brag about his day with the king and queen. *Haman recounted to them the glory of [the king's] riches..., and every instance where the king had magnified him... Haman also said, 'Even Esther the queen let no one but me come with the king to the banquet'"* (verses 11-12).

When Haman tells his listeners that Mordecai put a damper on his day by defying him, his wife and friends advise him to have the gallows prepared to hang him the next day. Then Haman would be able to go to the second banquet with great joy. Liking this idea, Haman determines to ask the king the next morning if he can hang Mordecai before the banquet. Even before that conversation, Haman had the gallows built.

LEARNING ALERT

According to Proverbs 16:18, pride goes before destruction. Another important truth is that God shares His glory with no one. Haman, however, is unaware of God and doesn't realize that his life is but a vapor and his time on earth is fleeting. Neither is Haman aware that God is sovereign, God is at work in the world, and God is the orchestra conductor of our lives. We are His servants, ever subject to His power and will.

Yet we are also children of the King, and we will one day be princes and princesses in heaven. Our days of glory will come, but now we serve. When God calls us, we go. When He grants us favor, we praise Him.

In *Mere Christianity*, C. S. Lewis wrote, "According to Christian teachers, the essential vice, the utmost evil, is pride. Unchastity, anger, greed, drunkenness, and all that, are mere flea bites in comparison."

When we call our friends together, it should be to recount God's glory, not our own.

Father, all glory resides in You!!! Amen!

Discussion Questions

1. Talk about a time or two when you felt you were bulletproof or when you had the world by the tail. What led to those feelings—and what brought you back to reality?

2. Since our lives are but a vapor, what is the most important thing you should be doing with your life?

3. Why is doing that particular thing—living with that particular thing as your top priority—difficult?

LESSON 40
The Tables Are Turned

Esther 6:1-10

During that night the king could not sleep so he gave an order to bring the book of records, the chronicles, and they were read before the king. It was found written what Mordecai had reported concerning Bigthana and Teresh, two of the king's eunuchs who were doorkeepers, that they had sought to lay hands on King Ahasuerus.

The king said, "What honor or dignity has been bestowed on Mordecai for this?" Then the king's servants who attended him said, "Nothing has been done for him." So the king said, "Who is in the court?" Now Haman had just entered the outer court of the king's palace in order to speak to the king about hanging Mordecai on the gallows which he had prepared for him.

The king's servants said to him, "Behold, Haman is standing in the court." And the king said, "Let him come in." So Haman came in and the king said to him, "What is to be done for the man whom the king desires to honor?" And Haman said to himself, "Whom would the king desire to honor more than me?"

Then Haman said to the king, "For the man whom the king desires to honor, let them bring a royal robe which the king has worn, and the horse on which the king has ridden, and on whose head a royal crown has been placed; and let the robe and the horse be handed over to one of the king's most noble princes and let them array the man whom the king desires to honor and lead him on horseback through the city square, and proclaim before him, 'Thus it shall be done to the man whom the king desires to honor.' "

Then the king said to Haman, "Take quickly the robes and the horse as you have said, and do so for Mordecai the Jew, who is sitting at the king's gate; do not fall short in anything of all that you have said." So Haman took the robe and the horse, and arrayed Mordecai, and led him on horseback through the city square, and proclaimed before him, "Thus it shall be done to the man whom the king desires to honor."
Esther 6:1-10

No chapter in the Bible displays God's sense of humor more than Esther 6. Wouldn't it have been fun to be a fly on the wall as the king and Haman had this conversation? God has clearly orchestrated events to humiliate the wicked and proud Haman. On the very day Haman anticipates the most glorious accomplishment of getting rid of Mordecai, he instead has a very bad day. A very, very, very bad day!

SWEET DREAMS

After his first banquet with Esther and the king—and before the second—Haman decides to build the gallows from which he would hang Mordecai. In the morning he would get the king to OK his evil deed. Haman falls asleep that night with great anticipation of the next day's events: he would hang his nemesis in the morning and then enjoy the honor of a banquet with the king and queen that afternoon.

As Haman dreams of those delights, the king has insomnia. So he calls his servants to read the kingdom's book of records. (Persians were known to keep very detailed records of all events.) The servants open the book and read... the story of Mordecai. Remember when Mordecai reported to the queen the plot to assassinate the king? Mordecai had saved the king's life.

> The king said [to his servants], "What honor or dignity has been bestowed on Mordecai for this?"
>
> Then the king's servants who attended him said replied, "Nothing has been done for him" (Esther 6:3).

NOW *THAT'S* AWKWARD!

The next morning Haman arrives at the palace to ask the king for permission to hang Mordecai. Before Haman can make his request, the king asks Haman, "What is to be done for the man whom the king desires to honor?" (verse 6).

Haman thinks, *The king must be talking about me!* So Haman goes big and speaks of this man wearing a robe the king has worn, riding a horse the king has ridden, and being led through the streets by one of the king's most noble princes. The king then tells Haman to do so for Mordecai the Jew (verse 10).

Now that's funny! Haman's shock and dismay must have been off the charts. You can't make this stuff up.

BETTER LUCK NEXT TIME

Obeying the king, Haman does for Mordecai all he had described thinking he was the one to be honored. Oh, how the mighty have fallen. After the parade, Haman covers his face in humiliation and goes home. It just can't get any worse than this.

As Haman mourns the day's events, the king's servants arrive to take him to the banquet. Maybe his day is about to improve...or maybe not.

Lord, thank you that you never rest. Instead, You are always working 'behind the scenes' to orchestrate Your plan for our lives. What peace we have knowing You are always with us. Father, we thank You that You protect us like a shepherd protects his sheep. And we thank You that You have promised to take us home to live with You forever. Amen!

Discussion Questions

1. What are some reasons being proud is a problem?

2. What perspective on ourselves and our achievements does God want us to have?

3. What can we do to live with a healthy confidence rather than pride?

LESSON 41
Esther Exposes Haman

Esther 7:1-6

Now the king and Haman came to drink wine with Esther the queen. And the king said to Esther on the second day also as they drank their wine at the banquet, "What is your petition, Queen Esther? It shall be granted you. And what is your request? Even to half of the kingdom it shall be done." Then Queen Esther replied, "If I have found favor in your sight, O king, and if it pleases the king, let my life be given me as my petition, and my people as my request; for we have been sold, I and my people, to be destroyed, to be killed and to be annihilated. Now if we had only been sold as slaves, men and women, I would have remained silent, for the trouble would not be commensurate with the annoyance to the king."

Then King Ahasuerus asked Queen Esther, "Who is he, and where is he, who would presume to do thus?" Esther said, "A foe and an enemy is this wicked Haman!" Then Haman became terrified before the king and queen.
Esther 7:1-6

WHAT A DAY!

Pride is a cruel and blinding master....

Yesterday Haman was on the top of the world. He gathered together his wife and friends and spoke in great detail of his greatness and accomplishments. This morning he had a significant set-back when the king chose to honor the man that Haman had hoped to hang.

But that was then, and this is now. Perhaps this afternoon will rebuild Haman's dignity as he dines with the king and queen.

FROM BAD TO WORSE

As the king and Haman drink wine at their private banquet with the queen, the king once again says, *"What is your petition, Queen Esther?"* (Esther 7:2). The king is still dizzy with love and affection for Esther. Her beauty and poise remain irresistible to him.

Esther takes a deep breath, whispers a prayer, and drops a bomb. She says, *"If I have found favor in your sight, O king, and if it pleases the king, let my life be given me as my petition and my people as my request; for we have been sold, I and my people, to be destroyed, to be killed and to be annihilated"* (verses 3-4).

Esther speaks with boldness and confidence. Her words echo the description of Haman's official document that had been distributed throughout the land: *"Letters were sent by courier to all the king's provinces to destroy, to kill and to annihilate all the Jews, both young and old, women and children, in one day, the thirteenth day of the twelve month"* (3:13).

Haman's brain must have exploded with fear. The king responds to Esther's report of this evil man: "*Who is he, and where is he, who would presume to do such?*" (verse 5).

Esther replies, "*A foe and enemy is this wicked Haman*" (verse 6).

HANG HIM HIGH!

The enraged king leaves the room, most likely on his way to get the guards. Haman takes the opportunity to beg the queen for mercy. When the king returns, the begging Haman appears to be on top of the queen.

Entering the room, the king bursts out, "*Will he even assault the queen with me in the house?*" (verse 8).

At that moment the guards seize Haman. One of the servants speaks to the king:

> "*The gallows [are] standing at Haman's house fifty cubits high, which Haman made for Mordecai, who spoke good on behalf of the king." And the king said, "Hang him on it." So they hanged Haman on the gallows which he had prepared for Mordecai, and the king's anger subsided.*" (verses 9-10)

GOD IS IN CONTROL

The book of Esther truly has all the elements of a screenplay with its villain, heroine, hero, deceit, intrigue, plotting, and a huge plot twist that was orchestrated by God and that plays out in real time as these actors watched.

Although God is never mentioned in the book of Esther, His presence could not be any clearer. He is God, and no enemy—spirit or flesh—will usurp His covenants or foil His plans. What man and Satan intend for evil, God uses for good. Yes, the happiness of our lives is blended with pain, trials, and challenges. But our experiences are never random or chance. We are not victims. God is in control!

LEARNING ALERT

You may be going through a very difficult time in life right now. You and your family may be going through some horrific circumstances. You might wonder where God is and why He's allowing this to happen. In such situations, we need God to enlarge our faith so as to see beyond the fog and cling to hope. He simply expects us to have faith in Him.

We don't know what tomorrow holds, but we do know who holds tomorrow. We can wholeheartedly trust God, knowing that everything about your journey and mine will unfold according to His good plan and in His perfect timing.

When Esther goes before the king after not being called for 30 days, she doesn't know how the king will respond. But she trusts that God will take care of her.

For many of God's people, a step of faith like the one Esther chooses has meant suffering, torture, and even death.

In such circumstances, we must remember that our physical death is not the end of our life. It's simply a bridge to a better, richer, more satisfying eternal life.

Father, You rule the events of our lives, whether good or seemingly bad. And in all these things, we overwhelmingly conquer through Jesus Christ, our Lord. Amen!

Discussion Questions

1. Why do you—or don't you—struggle to let God deal with those people who want to hurt you or who have hurt you?

2. Do you believe that God will protect you the way He protected Esther and Mordecai? Why or why not? Be specific.

LESSON 42
Surprise House Guest

Esther 8:1-7

> On that day King Ahasuerus gave the house of
> Haman, the enemy of the Jews, to Queen Esther;
> and Mordecai came before the king, for Esther had
> disclosed what he was to her. The king took off his signet
> ring which he had taken away from Haman and gave it
> to Mordecai. And Esther set Mordecai over the house of
> Haman.

> Then Esther spoke again to the king, fell at his feet, wept
> and implored him to avert the evil scheme of Haman the
> Agagite and his plot which he had devised against the
> Jews. The king extended the golden scepter to Esther. So
> Esther arose and stood before the king. Then she said,
> "If it pleases the king and if I have found favor before
> him and the matter seems proper to the king and I am
> pleasing in his sight, let it be written to revoke the letters
> devised by Haman, the son of Hammedatha the Agagite,
> which he wrote to destroy the Jews who are in all the
> king's provinces. For how can I endure to see the calamity
> which will befall my people, and how can I endure to see
> the destruction of my kindred?"

> So King Ahasuerus said to Queen Esther and to
> Mordecai the Jew, "Behold, I have given the house of
> Haman to Esther, and him they have hanged on the

gallows because he had stretched out his hands against the Jews."
Esther 8:1-7

ISN'T IT IRONIC?

By God's invisible, yet evident providence, Haman hanged on the gallows he himself had built. Isn't it ironic?

When Joseph's brothers sold him as a slave to a passing caravan, who could've known that Joseph would rise to second in command in Egypt and his brothers would eventually bow before him?

God is the Originator of irony. After all, what man intends for evil, God uses for good (see Genesis 50:20).

"HONEY, I'M HOME!"

On the day of Haman's death, King Ahasuerus gives Esther the house of Haman. The king also calls for Mordecai, for Esther has disclosed that he is her cousin.

When Mordecai stands before him, the king takes off *his signet ring which he had taken away from Haman and gave it to Mordecai. And Esther set Mordecai over the house of Haman* (Esther 8:2).

I suppose it will be something of a shock to Haman's wife when Mordecai walks into the house that evening and says, "Honey, I'm home!"

REVERSE THE IRREVERSIBLE

Meanwhile, although Esther is happy about the day's events, she is well aware that the command to slaughter the Jews is an irreversible edict. Nevertheless, falling at the king's feet, she weeps and begs for the edict to be reversed.

Although the king can't reverse it, he has a plan. The king calls in his scribes to work with Mordecai to draft a new decree, which he will seal with the king's signet ring.

This decree grants Jews the *right to assemble and defend their lives, to destroy, to kill and to annihilate the entire army of any people or province which might attack them* (verse 15). As a result of this glorious decree, *for the Jews there was light and gladness and joy and honor* (verse 16).

LEARNING ALERT

The book of James contrasts the proud and the humble: *God is opposed to the proud but gives grace to the humble.... Humble yourselves in the presence of the Lord, and He will exalt you* (4:6, 10). Proverbs 28:25 says, *An arrogant man stirs up strife, but he who trusts in the LORD will prosper.*

God instructs us, His children, to be poor in spirit by recognizing our need for Him. He also calls on us to be thankful. We see throughout the Bible that He is quickly angered by those who claim credit for what He has given them.

Our mission is clear: to serve God with humility and gratitude.

Lord, a happy ending is emerging for Esther and Mordecai's story. Our stories don't always end in happiness, and our trials often persist and persist. Nevertheless, You promise that "he who trusts in the LORD will prosper." Remind us that Your timing is not always our timing. Help us wait with faith, trust, humility, and patience as You, dear Lord, continue writing our stories. Help us remain strong, seek You, and follow You always. Amen!

Discussion Questions

1. What helps you trust God in bad times?

2. What are the key characteristics of humility? Which one should you prayerfully ask God to develop within you?

3. Why is it important for us to be thankful? Why is being grateful sometimes a hard thing to do? Give a couple reasons.

LESSON 43
Mordecai's Promotion

Esther 10:1-3

> *Now King Ahasuerus laid a tribute on the land and on the coastlands of the sea. And all the accomplishments of his authority and strength, and the full account of the greatness of Mordecai to which the king advanced him, are they not written in the Book of the Chronicles of the Kings of Media and Persia? For Mordecai the Jew was second only to King Ahasuerus, and great among the Jews and in favor with his many kinsmen, one who sought the good of his people and one who spoke for the welfare of his whole nation.* Esther 10:1-3

TRUE GREATNESS

On the day designated for the enemies of the Jews to attack and annihilate them, the absolute opposite takes place. Because of the king's edict, the Jews are well prepared and able not only to defend themselves but also to move offensively against their enemies. Esther 9:1 says, *"The Jews themselves gained the mastery over those who hated them.*

The unspoken God of the contrary continues to be intimately involved in the details of this reversal-of-fortune story: *No one could stand before [the Jews], for the dread of them had fallen on all the people* (verse 2). Having become well aware of the Jews' power and strength, people throughout the Persian Empire—whether enemies of the Jews or not—fell under their submission.

THE GREATNESS OF MORDECAI

And God has placed the godly and righteous Mordecai in this leadership position. In fact, people who are neutral in this conflict line up to support the Jews *because the dread of Mordecai had fallen on them. Indeed, Mordecai was great in the king's house, and his fame spread throughout the provinces; for the man Mordecai became greater and greater* (verse 4).

Just as God allowed Joseph and Daniel to be great in the earthly kingdoms of Egypt and Babylon, respectively, God raises up Mordecai in Persia. In each of these three examples, God puts in position a man who can influence the king and preserve His chosen people and the line of the Messiah.

Hear this tribute to Mordecai in the last verse of Esther: *Mordecai the Jew was second only to the king, and great among the Jews and in favor with many of his kinsman, one who sought the good of his people and one who spoke for the welfare of his whole nation* (10:3).

WHAT KIND OF MAN IS HE?

God was going to use someone to influence the king and emerge as a leader of the nation in order to preserve the Jews. So what kind of man was God looking for? A man who was concerned with the welfare of others over himself. A man who, if he attained wealth, power, and fame, would remain humble and focused on the welfare of his people. A man who would remember his role as a servant of God. In the time of the Persian Empire, this man was Mordecai.

And Mordecai knew that only because of God was he in this position of prominence. Mordecai didn't fall prey to the temptation to think that his greatness was because of something within himself. Nor did he take credit for navigating his life and attaining such greatness. No, Mordecai knew that his position and power were completely from God and completely for the benefit of God's people. Mordecai knew God was using him to accomplish an important eternal-kingdom outcome.

Whatever our station in life, we are to be stewards of what God has given us, as Esther and Mordecai model for us. Like the two of them, when God gives you much, be ready to give all in return. Be ready for *such a time as this*, ready to obey and do what God has created and called you to do.

LEARNING ALERT

I love this story for many reasons, but what's the big takeaway? For me, that big takeaway is that this historical account is more than a fairytale. These events actually happened, giving us an example of faith in action. Esther and Mordecai show us how to live—in open communication with God—a life that glorifies Him.

Lord, may we learn from Esther and Mordecai. May we learn courage, faith, and resolve, qualities that all of us can aspire to and, by Your power, live out day by day. May we be faithful servants, Lord God! Amen!

Discussion Questions

1. What is your main takeaway from the book of Esther? What other significant lessons or observations do you want to hold on to?

2. What do you think God has prepared or is preparing you for, through this study? Be as specific as you can.

3. What did you learn from watching Esther's faith in action?

CHAPTER 9

WHAT'S NEXT?

Are you ready to go deeper with God and meet with him daily? I hope you will join me on a quest to live out our faith daily and find our purpose and passion in God's written word.

I've been a Christian for a long time, but I began this journey into a deeper walk with God in December 2015 when my pastor challenged me to take my faith to the next level and spend dedicated time EVERY DAY with God.

It would be an honor for you to join me on a daily walk toward a dynamic relationship with God. It is my daily prayer that I am able to help you on your journey by providing a foundation of faith, wisdom, resulting in a more energized life filled with joy, purpose and meaning.

TAKE THE FIRST STEP

The Journey to live out your faith daily begins with a prayer and a pledge. Use your own words but I encourage you to pray along this pattern:

Father, by faith I want to take a step forward toward a closer walk with you. I ask that you help me move beyond having a faith that is relegated to only certain aspects of my life. Move me toward a genuine faith that is fully integrated with all aspects of my life, personal and professional. Grant me the grace to grow my faith in You one day at a time. Amen!

In I Samuel 12, Jonathan made a pledge to David. Verse 16 says, *"So Jonathan made this agreement with David and his family, and he asked the Lord to hold them responsible for keeping it."*

Once again, with God's help, use your own words but I encourage you to make a pledge along this pattern:

With God's help, I commend myself to God to make progress daily toward a closer walk with Him. My walk will be strengthened as I take in a little of God's Word daily, share my learnings with close Christian friends and family and apply my biblical insights to daily living and decisions.

Now you are ready to take your next steps in this journey. Your journey encompasses three key elements:

1. Daily Time with God

2. Daily accountability with friends and family

3. Make better decisions Daily

Reminder: Doing this "daily" is a worthwhile goal but it is not an exercise in legalism. Doing it 'daily' is an aspiration not a requirement. You may want to begin with a goal of 3 to 5 days a week and build it from there.

1. **Daily Time with God**. Once you have made the decision to spend time daily with God, I encourage you to follow the pattern of READ, REFLECT and WRITE. You can follow the 3Rs in a 10-15-minute timeframe or up to an hour or more. I started out at 20 minutes and now spend 45–60 minutes daily.

   a. <u>Read</u> – Pick a Bible book and determine to read through it little by little each day. Don't rush it. Take it slow and think more in terms of reading paragraphs or sections rather than reading chapters. Reading through books is better than just haphazardly picking verses. Books I recommend as you begin are Luke, John, Philippians, Ruth, Esther, 1 Samuel. Also, you can do sections in Psalms or Proverbs (such as chapter 1-5, etc.)

   b. After you have read a section, now focus some time on <u>Reflection</u>. This is time to prayerfully ask God for wisdom and insight; ask and reflect on what the key message is. What does this teach us about mankind and/or what about the nature of God? Does it call us to act or think differently? What should we learn? Be prayerful and reflective.

c. Finally, <u>w**R**ite</u> something down. For many years I would only read and reflect. But it was not until I disciplined myself to write daily, that the Word of God took on a deeper meaning than ever before. There are no rules about what to write. Just start writing, even if you feel you have nothing to say. Ask questions, make observations, write out applications, etc. I have found that writing opens me up to insights that I didn't get by just reading and reflecting. This is a very powerful and impactful step

2. **Daily Accountability Partner**

a. Who is a reliable Christian friend or family member that you can partner with? Ask them if you can text them after you have your daily time with God with just a sentence or two about what you wrote down.

b. I followed this texting process with my Pastor in 2015 when I began and continued for 6 months until it was a habit. I expanded it to include my wife, a few close friends and my men's Bible Study group. Now I have a small but growing blog following.

3. **Daily decisions and actions**

a. It's very easy to have a wonderful time alone with God in the morning and then not think of Him all day.

b. Give yourself triggers or reminders throughout the day so that you can keep what you learned in the morning at the forefront of your mind throughout the day.

c. Record actions or decisions you made that seem to be directly related to what you are learning from God's Word.

You are now ready to begin the journey of a lifetime. Sign up for my blog and keep me posted on how you are progressing.

For additional resources from Larry Shaffer, including more devotionals, visit larryshafferblog.com